A Lesbian's Awakening to Purpose, Self-Love, and God

A Soul's Journey to Self-Awareness, Identity, and Truth

THE REVEREND LISA R. KELSON

BALBOA.PRESS

A DIVISION OF HAY HOUSE

Copyright © 2022 The Reverend Lisa R. Kelson.

All rights reserved. No part of this book may be used or reproduced by any means, graphic, electronic, or mechanical, including photocopying, recording, taping or by any information storage retrieval system without the written permission of the author except in the case of brief quotations embodied in critical articles and reviews.

Balboa Press books may be ordered through booksellers or by contacting:

Balboa Press
A Division of Hay House
1663 Liberty Drive
Bloomington, IN 47403
www.balboapress.com
844-682-1282

Because of the dynamic nature of the Internet, any web addresses or links contained in this book may have changed since publication and may no longer be valid. The views expressed in this work are solely those of the author and do not necessarily reflect the views of the publisher, and the publisher hereby disclaims any responsibility for them.

The author of this book does not dispense medical advice or prescribe the use of any technique as a form of treatment for physical, emotional, or medical problems without the advice of a physician, either directly or indirectly. The intent of the author is only to offer information of a general nature to help you in your quest for emotional and spiritual well-being. In the event you use any of the information in this book for yourself, which is your constitutional right, the author and the publisher assume no responsibility for your actions.

Any people depicted in stock imagery provided by Getty Images are models, and such images are being used for illustrative purposes only.
Certain stock imagery © Getty Images.

Scripture quotations are taken from the Revised Standard Version of the Bible, copyright © 1946, 1952, 1971 by the Division of Christian Education of the National Council of the Churches of Christ in the USA. Used by permission.

Scripture quotations are taken from the Holy Bible, New International Version®. NIV®. Copyright © 1973, 1978, 1984 by International Bible Society. Used by permission of Zondervan. All rights reserved.

Print information available on the last page.

ISBN: 979-8-7652-3417-4 (sc)
ISBN: 979-8-7652-3418-1 (hc)
ISBN: 979-8-7652-3419-8 (e)

Library of Congress Control Number: 2022922167

Balboa Press rev. date: 01/03/2023

My deepest gratitude is to my mother and father. To my mother, Elanor Burbank Amos, thank you for teaching me to follow my own path in life and for encouraging me to live into my most authentic self. Mom, thank you for leading the cause on equality, morality, and justice issues long before they became popular and for instilling their importance in each of your daughters. Thank you for teaching us how to be courageous in the midst of injustice and difficult times and how to rely on our inner strength. To my father, Charles M. Kelson III, thank you for teaching me the importance of keeping it moving in life when the earth crumbles under your feet. Thank you for ingraining the importance of developing personal character and the importance of humor and humility as we walk this sacred journey. To my sisters, Laura, Nancy, and Tammy, thank you for supporting and sharing this journey of awakening with me.

CONTENTS

PREFACE

My hope in writing this book is to share my journey with others who are struggling to find and embrace their true authentic self. To find our purpose, we must also find that part of us that is divinely inspired. Finding that spark will allow the soul to live a purposeful and meaningful life. Living from the soul's divine spark will offer plenty of opportunities to grow and evolve into that person you were ordained to become. Living from any other perspective will not fulfill and expand the soul who has come here seeking enlightenment and to live a purposeful experience.

It has taken me nearly sixty years to wake up to my true authentic self as a lesbian. In my younger days, I had no idea that there was a deeper and higher self waiting to be discovered. For many years, I lived from my lower aspect while trying to fit into society's social rules and norms. I ignored my inner compass and became frustrated because I did not fit into the labels, dogma, and the traditional path. Falling in love with a woman would force me to examine family and religious teachings. At the time, I didn't realize that it would be this path that would lead me to a spiritual awakening. Once I realized that there was a spiritual path, I immersed myself in the higher teachings, and it would be this spiritual path that led my soul to freedom.

I hope this book will give you the courage to live into that person you came here to embody. Let nothing hold you back from living into that divine spark of love who came here to expand and offer the world a radiant light of love and difference. Love is love.

ACKNOWLEDGMENTS

We are never alone on our earthbound journey. We planned this journey with our soul tribe. Nothing happens by chance. Our lives are interwoven with people who are here for the purpose of teaching us, guiding us, inspiring us, and loving us as we embrace this journey called life. Spiritually and energetically, we are all connected to the One Source that gives everything life. We are all cocreating together.

With that said, I want to thank all the teachers in my life who believed in me, supported me, and offered me love until I was able to find my own voice and inner power. The first person that I would like to thank is my first partner, Cathy Cason, who lovingly showed me that God is love and any judgment that falls outside these parameters is not God or love. Thank you for helping me to embrace the person I came here to be.

More recently, I want to thank my professors at the Episcopal Divinity School who worked tirelessly to see that I achieved academic success. Thank you, Aura A. Fluet, the librarian who was always available on a Friday afternoon. Thank you, Gale Yee, for rigorous writing assignments that challenged me, and Patrick Cheng, for helping me expand my discussion points. Thank you to my writing professor, Lucretia Yaghjian, for helping me "sing my song," and Larry Wills for listening and valuing my inputs and teaching me the art of exegetical work. Kwok Pui Lan, I am forever grateful for your spiritual guidance and your intuitive awareness and knowledge of my deeper self. Thank you for teaching me to honor the challenges in my life. Thank you for the many affirmations that encouraged me to believe in myself. Moreover, thank you for teaching me how to grow spiritually and how to embrace my differences. Julie Lytle, thank you for walking with me as I grew into my higher self. Thank you for your vision and success of implementing a community distance learning program and filling it with community and love.

I also want to thank my cohort group of 2011 for assisting me during this profound spiritual and academic experience. Your kindness and gentle support provided a loving foundation, family, friendship, and support. Thank you for carrying me until I was able to fly. I also want to offer appreciation to Danny Barnes, Balboa Press's senior publishing consultant, for her passion in bestowing spiritual enlightenment books to the LGBTQ+ community for the purpose of nourishing them as they walk the arduous path of finding themselves in a world that can seem so difficult. Thank you for believing, encouraging, and stretching me to become a writer who delivers hope to those in search of their authentic self. Lastly, thank you, Stefanie Palma, for the time spent on editing and proofing the draft manuscript and Dee Thomas for covering the pulpit in my absence.

INTRODUCTION

My life's purpose is to assist others in awakening their souls to divine love and truth. As the soul awakens, it gradually begins to grow and expand. This expansion leads the soul to the liberation of its higher self.

As awareness expands, the soul begins a journey to awaken its authentic self. This journey is an intuitive path and is spiritual in nature. This path is one of light, love, acceptance, and forgiveness. To ascend on this path, the soul must gain enlightenment, knowledge of self, and higher consciousness.

As the soul awakens, it begins to understand itself and its purpose for incarnation. These reasons fluctuate depending on the soul's desire. Some souls come to learn lessons while other souls come to assist humanity in their great spiritual awakening. Our experiences here on earth provide us with many opportunities to expand and learn how to love.

Our higher selves beckon the soul to awaken to its authentic self. That spark that God created long ago. An awakening requires that we embrace the concept that we are one with source. We are never alone or separated. To know thyself is to liberate thyself. To free the soul, it must awaken to its divine state as God originally intended.

Life on earth provides the soul with many experiences in hopes that it will awaken and return to God. The soul must learn how to discern truth from fiction. This task can be difficult in human form. We are inundated with ages of ancestral, social, and religious belief ideology. The liberation of the soul requires a deconstruction of old beliefs that are no longer serving us. We must begin to embrace new understandings about the laws and principals of life. These new understandings will assist the soul's ascent in higher consciousness that is needed for the soul to mature. Our souls must awaken before we are able to grasp higher knowledge.

I traveled this same path. In my early days, I succumbed to the patriarchal teachings of the Catholic church and their influence on my father's family's religious beliefs and social norms. Intended or not, these standards taught me that boys were more valuable than girls. I didn't understand at the time. I felt less valuable and unwanted at times. I just wanted to spend time with my father. At that age, something inside me needed to feel special and loved by him.

My father's family's rigid social norms around gender identity and gender expression were only the beginning of my experience as a lesbian. These social norms continued as I grew up. I tried to assimilate into these rigid social norms. In doing so, I also was suffocating that person God had created. I fell in love and was soon confronted head on with my identity as a lesbian. This path eventually led my soul to liberation.

I hope this book will be an inspiration to many who are struggling to embrace their authentic selves around sexual orientation to include all those who identify outside binary social norms. I also hope that this book can assist parents and others who work with children who identify as LGBTQ+. These children will need a foundation of love and acceptance to help them grow into the person they feel called to be, whatever that may look like.

CHAPTER ONE

Early Life

It has taken me nearly sixty years to find, believe, and then embrace my true authentic self. I spent half of my life learning who I am at the soul level. Once I learned I was created and loved by God, and I had a divine purpose in this world, it not only liberated me but encouraged me to become the person who my soul intended. This liberation allowed me to release all my fears and embrace my true identity as a lesbian. This liberation allowed me to meet a God who I had never before embraced. A God full of love, purpose, and meaning for my life.

My hope is to reach other lesbian, gay, bisexual, transgender, and queer (LGBTQ+) people who are struggling to accept themselves as uniquely created and loved by God. This acceptance will help fulfill a purpose in their life. This list includes all people who may feel outcast as a result of gender or sexual-identity norms. This includes people who may identify as asexual, intersex, or pansexual. It also includes, but is not limited to, those who identify as gender-nonconforming or gender-fluid people.

Embracing our true identity is essential to living our best life. The soul creates an optimal plan. When the soul embarks on following this optimal plan in life, it will thrive. Living into our divine identity will optimize the soul's chance of evolving into its higher self. This optimal path will provide the soul with the necessary experiences and nourishment that are required to achieve a healthy, happy, and balanced life. Choosing to live a life short of the soul's higher intent would be spiritual death for the soul. The soul's goal is to evolve in each incarnation to its higher aspect. Every incarnation offers the soul opportunities to ascend higher. This is possible only when we begin to recognize the soul's guidance and prompting.

Where It All Began

I was born in Pensacola, Florida, a small town in the far western panhandle of north Florida. I was born to Charles M. Kelson III and Elanor Burbank Amos. My parents were high school sweethearts who dated while attending a technical high school. My father was enrolled in the body and fender program, while Mom was enrolled in the beautician program, a typical gender-binary curriculum. He was seventeen and she was sixteen.

Their affection for each other grew daily as they spent time together mainly during their school day. Their high school experience was focused on accomplishing their respective programs to meet graduation requirements. Like many people in relationships who are attempting to finish their education, they lacked adequate quality time with each other.

If the constraints of achieving graduation requirements weren't enough, my maternal grandmother managed to impose very strict dating rules that kept my mother tethered to the house. Nevertheless, there were a few occasions when they actually spent some time outside school. One of these times was when Dad drove Mom to school. Other times included when Mom managed to coordinate social meetups around town at friends' birthday parties or trips to the movies.

As their relationship evolved, they soon fell in love and Mom became pregnant. Because of oppressive cultural norms during this time, they both had to quit high school. Mom was not allowed to attend school while she was pregnant. This necessitated Dad to secure employment for the purpose of supporting his new family.

Fortunately, my great uncle owned an electrical business and agreed to employ my father as a "shop boy." My father's term. The shop boy was responsible for cleaning the shop office, unloading trucks, and putting materials away. The position was contingent on him completing high school. Dad honored my uncle's request by completing an adult program at night. With my uncle's help, he soon completed the state's requirements to ascertain his journeyman electrical license.

During this time, my father's parents gave him a small trailer to live in. Dad remembers it being tiny, pink, and white. I have a black-and-white picture of Mom sitting on the entrance steps with her beloved dog. My twin sister, Laura, and I were born in 1962 while we were living in that memorable trailer. Mom describes their living quarters as very cramped. She remembers it being so small they had to give up their double bed to make room for the baby beds.

Laura and I lived in this cramped trailer with our parents until our family house was built. My paternal grandfather gave my dad some property so that he could build our house. Dad mentioned to me the entire family participated in constructing the new house. My father said it took one year to build. Our family had professional plumbers, electricians, carpenters, and other tradespersons needed to complete the house. We moved in when my twin sister and I were around one year of age.

By the time we were three, our family had grown in size to a total of six. Mom delivered my two younger sisters, Nancy and Tammy, in 1964 and 1965 respectively. Their arrival completed our family.

Early Childhood

We settled in our new home and began the sentient aspect of life as a family. These early experiences would become critical in developing and shaping my foundational understanding around ethics and social norms. This included sexuality, sexual orientation, gender norms, and gender expression.

The relationships we form while here on earth provide our souls with exceptional learning experiences. These circumstances are vast and by design. They will stretch the soul's awareness about itself and its relationship with the divine. As the soul cocreates, it begins to find its true authentic self as God designed. All relationships, both good and bad, provide the incarnate soul with unique learning opportunities. While family interrelationships can be dysfunctional, tumultuous, and painful at times, they provide the soul with diverse situations that cultivate a rich environment needed to challenge the soul.

By nature, relationships can be emotional and arduous. However, it is this very facet that propels the soul to achieve its desired lessons. These embodied lessons provide the soul with authentic encounters that help the soul awaken to its identity, purpose, and growth. I can't stress the impact that our family's experiences have had on teaching us lessons we came here to learn. It may be difficult to embrace the concept that our soul learns valuable lessons as a result of dysfunctional and tumultuous situations.

Our childhood experiences can oscillate from soul to soul. There are some souls who experience healthy relationships with their parents. In homes where love prevails, relationships and deep bonds are created. Contrarily, souls who experience a lack of love, empathy, and compassion have an opportunity to use this negative experience and build healthier, more loving relationships. The soul often becomes more loving and compassionate to others when it has experienced harsh relationship experiences.

My experiences were no different. I lived through many uncomfortable situations as I grew up. These experiences would shape me and eventually force me to reconcile my sexual identity with God. There is power in the unveiling. Although my mom visualized a family unit that would spend quality time together, her ideal family life would end in a turbulent divorce.

I remember when they filed for divorce. I was in the second grade and had used this news as my show-and-tell story for that day. The teacher quickly ushered me to my seat and promptly called Mom to tell her what I had done. I don't know why I felt the need to share this delicate information in front of my class peers. I think deep down I was grieving. I didn't want to lose either one of my parents. I had grown accustomed to seeing them every day in my life. I didn't know what to expect.

It was a traumatic experience for me as a child. I felt my world was falling apart. The very foundation where I stood was disintegrating. The fractured family unit created feelings of emptiness, disconnection, loneliness, and disharmony.

This is one of those situations where culturally men were taught their role in the family was to provide basic food, shelter, and clothing. Stereotypically, nurturing, housework, and cooking would come from mothers. It was a difficult adjustment not having our father in our lives twenty-four-seven, but of course, we adjusted and began seeing him just on weekends. Over the next several years, the four of us would oscillate back and forth between Mom and Dad's primary homes as we tried desperately to look for a new normal.

Speaking for myself, I think I just wanted to feel love and experience a sense of connection again. Maybe I, too, was missing that family unity that Mom tried so desperately to wield together.

Sometimes growing up in a divorce family can be painful and difficult for children. I have heard many children express their feelings of separation and not feeling loved. This can cause a void deep inside them, making them feel isolated to the world. Often children blame themselves for their parents' divorce. They feel a tremendous responsibility for the breakup and for their parents' actions.

While negotiating this tumultuous experience, some children can become depressed and despondent. Some children of divorced parents must learn how to process their emotions of hurt and pain around the tumultuous experience. As a way to process their feelings, some children may begin to numb them through means of addiction, behavioral issues, low self-esteem, or they can even become despondent and withdrawn in school and home life. These experiences test our resolve and challenge us to examine our own identity. It makes us ask the hard questions about who we really are without our parents cohabitating.

It is a widely accepted belief that children select their parents just before birth. After embracing this concept, I began thinking retrospectively as to why I chose my parents. Believe it or not, the soul grows as it struggles to make sense out of life's chaotic conditions. The feelings I felt during those turbulent times would shape and mold my self-identity and self-worth. More to the point, these tumultuous experiences would force me to figure out who I was at soul level.

Prebirth planning might be a difficult concept to embrace, but the soul incarnates for the purpose of growing and learning. To accomplish our soul's desired learning requires the help of our soul family. It is understood that we travel together as a soul group and, as we come into this life, each agree to take on roles as mothers, fathers, sisters, brothers, grandparents, and other extended family members for the purpose of teaching and learning. We have been in many relations with each other over the eons.

With this understanding, I thoughtfully considered my soul's desired learning choices for this life. I came to the understanding that my soul's desire was to learn self-reliance, self-love, strength, and courage to live authentically.

Family dynamics are influential in helping to provide the soul with desired lessons. We learn lessons by having desired qualities missing in our chosen living experience. In other words, if the soul seeks to learn strength and self-reliance, it will plan a life that focuses on an outcome or goal of strength and self-reliance. To accomplish this, the soul will pick scenarios that will almost guarantee an outcome of its desired lesson. For example, my parents' divorce caused me to become stronger, more self-reliant, and more courageous.

Each time we incarnate our relationships with one another will change. This helps to balance karma and the soul's energy. Experiencing both the feminine and masculine energy helps the soul learn how to balance its creative energies. A balanced state is the most desirous.

Gender Norms, Social Norms, and Ethical Norms

By design, families teach us right from wrong. Parents, grandparents, aunts, uncles, and other family members teach us right moral conduct. These beliefs become entrenched in our ideological understanding about ethics and social norms in life. These social learnings become our core belief system. Typically, children believe what their parents believe, especially in their young lives. Their beliefs normally will not change unless a value is challenged. This is exactly how it unfolded for me.

My paternal grandmother and grandfather lived behind our property, which means they were very involved in our lives. As a matter of fact, the entire block was family. My grandfather sold the land to his children and to his brother's children. I remember my grandmother telling the girls to sit up tall and act politely. My paternal grandparents were very much steeped in traditional social and gender norms. Women had their roles in family and were to be subordinate to men in public. Men were the decision-makers in the family and in society. Men became husbands, and husbands were expected to provide financially for their wives and family. Boys were valued more than girls and given more latitude.

This belief structure collided with my mother's more egalitarian outlook of gender social norms. She is a very outspoken individual and has always held very strong beliefs pertaining to equal rights and equal opportunity. As a matter of fact, she informed my dad that if they had a son, he would take his turn in washing dishes. Of course, my father was appalled at the thought of his son performing a woman's job. My mother has a strong personality, and fortunately for my dad this situation never came up.

However, what did present itself were the times when my sisters and I wanted to go fishing with our dad. My mom would drive us to where my father was and negotiate with my dad for us to go along. My father would tell her that the men were going fishing, to which my mom would remark, "Yeah, their dad, grandfather, and cousin."

High School and College Offer

My two other sisters and I eventually began investing our time in sports. Sports would provide us an outlet from our chaotic home life. We began playing on community athletic teams. My younger sister began playing basketball on community leagues, and my twin sister and I played on a community softball team. I do remember my father making some of the practices and games while we were at the community level. I remember him in the stands getting my twin sister and me confused. It was difficult to tell us apart as we all had the same clothes and were wearing helmets. Mom was very involved with this facet of our lives. She ran the concession stand frequently and watched our games from the stand. She also made sure that we had the equipment needed to sponsor the sport.

As we grew, we eventually reached high school and began immersing ourselves in the various sports offered. I played both volleyball and softball. My younger sister played basketball and softball. My twin sister also played softball. This was a fun time because for the first time, the three of us were on the same high school softball team. I didn't realize it at the time, but these softball days would become very meaningful as we were able to spend time together on the softball field. Our team and coach became family and a mentor. This experience provided me with a sense of connection that I had long desired since the divorce. These people and the sport provided me with a way to bond with people in a more meaningful way.

I didn't realize it at the time, but my softball coach would become an influential role model for me and our team. She taught us how to access our inner strength. She provided us with hard-core, real-life lessons such as how to dig deep, especially when we felt we had nothing left to give. At practice, we always found the grit to sprint one more wind sprint, run one more lap, or run the stadium stairs one more time.

The stadium stairs were steeper than the height of my short legs but a great analogy to learning how to accomplish life's deeper problems. I remember having to compensate my stride in order to negotiate the stairs. I learned to swing my legs to the side so that I could clear the next step.

She introduced us to an inner strength that we didn't realize existed. This new knowledge helped us build a more confident belief structure. We now had the tools not only to run one more lap but suddenly were preparing to negotiate life's complexities. Back then, I didn't see the importance of all this hard-core work, but I soon realized that this experience wasn't just about softball and our win/loss record. It was about preparing us mentally, psychologically, and physically for life's future impediments.

Softball just happened to be the instrument used to begin preparing me for life's challenges later. As a result, I became strong and courageous. My softball experience would also serve as a platform to begin figuring out who I really was at the soul level. As a teenager, I had no idea who I was at a deeper level. I considered myself a loner with few friends. I was not popular and lacked confidence not only in my athletic abilities but also in my academic capacity. I was considered an average student. At that time, it seemed those ahead of me understood life and who they were. They seemed to have direction in their lives. Perhaps they seemed more secure of their personal identity and purpose.

At the very core of each of us is a power that resides within us, but it takes tenacity to figure it out. I also believe that we are more than our physical bodies or our situations. It takes a willingness to explore our inner selves at a spiritual level or soul level. Inward reflection will assist in accessing divine knowledge, purpose, identity, and divine intuition. It is impossible to complete our purpose here on earth unless we learn how to dig deep to access that divine spark within us. Accessing this power will lead us to the reason and purpose for our coming here. Life is very much about rising to the challenges of everyday life. It takes strength, courage, and the divine power within us to help accomplish our call. Retreating will not advance our soul's purpose and growth. It takes grit and a hard-core drive to dig deep within our core being to uncover that person that God created us to be. This will does not come from our own power; it comes from universal source or God.

My high school athletic experience, particularly softball, would pave the road for my next experience in life. Soren Kierkegaard said, "Life can only be understood backwards; but it must be lived forwards." How true this is. As I look back, I can see the very plan that my soul planned for the purpose of learning and growing in the classroom called earth.

Immediately after high school graduation, my twin sister and I registered for a softball tournament. The tournament was located in a remote place far north of town in an obscure wooded area off the main highway. A rutted, clay road led to the field where we all gathered to practice. The details are hazy, but the impact was life changing. Out of nowhere, a stranger walked up to both my twin sister and me as we were in the outfield and offered each of us a softball scholarship. Accepting the offer would require moving south for a couple of years.

I didn't hesitate! I accepted her offer immediately. The stranger would become my new coach and friend for two years. She told me to pack my bags and be ready to travel in two weeks. It was an exciting time for me. For some reason, I was not afraid of pursuing this endeavor. I just knew this was the path for me. My soul embraced this decision with ease, as if I had planned it long before I got here. I met the opportunity with excitement. The scholarship was offered by a small junior college in Fort Myers, Florida. My scholarship paid for my education but books and tuition only. I would need a job to support my living expenses.

I applied and was accepted for a work/study position at the college. The position required me to maintain the softball field. This entailed cutting the grass, dragging the infield clay, and using a roller to flatten any inconsistency in the outfield terrain. This opportunity was one of those life-changing moments, and I immediately recognized the value of my scholarship. I knew this opportunity had the power to change my life drastically. It would allow me to achieve a college education and that accomplishment would open many doors that were inaccessible before. I had never imagined in my wildest dreams that going to college was possible. My near future looked brighter. College was never discussed in my family; therefore, I assumed it was not possible. My parents did not have the money to send us to college so I accepted my circumstances.

This is an example of what we can achieve when we embrace that person that God created us to be. Initially, I accepted two beliefs: that I wasn't smart enough to go to college and that I could never afford college. To be honest, I never considered college as an option in my life because I felt it was beyond my reach. I would not understand this until later, but my soul had a different plan. This scholarship was just the beginning of the path that my soul had planned. My soul wanted the experience of learning new and different things. Our higher selves plan a life full of learning experiences; however, to take full advantage of this, we must learn how to listen and follow God, our soul, and higher self.

We have a life force energy deep within us. This power is called "prana" in Ayurveda. This power can also be called the awakened Christ in Christianity. It is a magical power that provides us with spiritual energy and knowledge about our spiritual path. This power sits and waits for us to set it free. This can be accomplished by releasing anything that is no longer serving us and by embracing spiritual understanding outside the confines of standard religious dogma. Any religion that focuses too much on dogmatic theology constructed around laws and traditions leaves us trapped in our rational mind. The rational mind is not capable of awakening our spiritual side.

Intuition and soul knowing are accessed through our spiritual power. This knowing guides us to the purpose as to why we came here. We can access this deeper knowing through meditation, higher awareness exercises, and intuition. All of this resides in our higher soul. What happens to so many is they never live into that higher plan that would light the way for the evolved soul. We settle for an average life and an average identity because we refuse to believe that we could become so much more. We settle for mediocracy when we are capable of achieving bliss. I followed my soul, and it eventually led me to a spiritual awakening; however, it has taken my entire life to figure this out. I wish that I had understood this sooner. My softball scholarship was a part of this plan; however, I would not understand this until much later.

A New Town

I settled into my new town and acquired a daily routine around school, work, and softball. My new teammates and coach became my new family. This opportunity seemed surreal. I couldn't believe that I was actually living a dream come true. It just felt right. I was on a spiritual high. I connected well with my new softball teammates. Eventually we all ended up sharing a house, which was beneficial to our finances. I took a small room that might resemble an enclosed porch. While it lacked central heating and air, I preferred the space because it provided me with quiet time and alone time. Even in my younger years, I preferred my space. As I said, I worked a part-time job at night to support my living expenses. This experience provided me with a wonderful bunch of people who embraced me as their own. These friends would end up being lifelong friends, and they remain in my heart to this day. We travel in soul groups so who knows? Perhaps we already knew each other prior to arriving in the physical and that is why we connected so well. I don't really know, but what I do know is that this was my path. The experience felt good to the soul.

The two years that I attended this particular community college flew by, but God always seemed to put people on my path to help me when I found myself struggling. For example, my English teacher was concerned when I failed to hand in homework lessons. She scheduled an appointment with me and was really concerned that my afterschool work schedule was negatively influencing my ability to complete her homework assignments. I remember her asking me when there was time for schoolwork. I had never met a teacher who was so concerned about a student's academic performance. She really cared about my struggles, and she wanted to help me achieve something more in life. I wasn't just a student to her. I was a special soul who needed extra help and some grace.

Without her guidance and tutoring, I would have failed English. At one point, the academic dean called for a meeting with my softball coach and me. In this conference, I was told that I was placed on academic probation. I had one semester to improve my grades or I would lose my softball scholarship.

At this point, my softball coach took me aside and began to teach me how to study. She taught me how to make flash cards and then would quiz me. We studied together initially until I was able to study on my own. Thereafter, I was capable of studying and preparing my own study cards. This small adjustment in my study habits helped me improve my academic standing, and I was eventually removed from the school's academic probation list. These are the critical experiences in our lives that define who we are. At this critical moment, I had a choice. I could have given up and convinced myself that I wasn't good enough or smart enough to attend college, or I could believe that I was there for a reason that was much bigger.

There will always be difficulties and hurdles to clear along our earthly journey. This journey was never meant to be easy. Our souls learn and grow when we face adversities in our lives. We have to believe in our passion and purpose and go for it. Never believe that you are sent here to accomplish your call and purpose alone. Learn the ancient technique of going within your heart center to connect with the divine. Divine source offers us a power greater than our own. This power is what nourishes us and feeds us stamina, wisdom, and love. God and your guides are with you every step of the way. You are never alone. Never buy into this pattern of thinking that you are alone. Learn to draw strength from your angels and guides for daily guidance.

Most of us never live into that person God created us to be because we don't ascribe to the belief that God has a greater version of us waiting for us to discover. Never give up! We are so much more powerful when we learn how to harness God's power and follow the soul's direction. My time in Fort Myers flew by. It was not an easy time. I struggled. Nothing worthwhile is given to us on a silver platter. I learned and saw all kinds of new and unique experiences that would stretch my belief system. This experience as a student, athlete, and worker allowed me to interact with all types of people.

I had grown fond of many people while I was there, even the head maintenance person who spent time getting the lawnmower unstuck when I inadvertently got it stuck in the trees and ditches.

I had met many wonderful people there and was really torn about my decision to return home. I had developed meaningful relationships where I felt connected and loved. It was here that I was first introduced to the LGBTQ+ lifestyle. For the first time, I had come face-to-face with a bias of my Catholic upbringing. I was taught that the gay lifestyle was wrong and that these people were an abomination and destined to hell. The word *abomination* is used by mainstream religion to scare people into conforming to rigid cultural norms. The God that I finally embraced was a God who loves unconditionally. All my Catholic teachings were imploding in my mind. I thought, *God must love me if God is love and loves unconditionally. God cannot be both love and evil. God is 100 percent divine love. God created each one of us and blessed our own uniqueness. God is a loving God.*

A metaphysical understanding of the word *abomination* describes erroneous thoughts, beliefs, and behaviors not in alignment with the divine. An abomination is believing restrictive and false beliefs that we retain from our childhood teachings. These come from our parents, grandparents, religion, and societal norms. *Abomination* references our lower personalities that act in alignment with our egos. The ego is not in alignment with the divine. Truth resides in the higher vibrations of divine love, and this is where we go to achieve higher consciousness and knowing.

I would not reconcile the topic of gay sexuality until another thirty years when I found myself falling in love with a woman. More on this later.

Most of us believe what our parents, grandparents, and religious doctrine teach us. We follow other people's beliefs and assume they have all the answers, and this simply is not true. It takes courage to follow your own truth, but your soul will never lie to you. We all must work to discover the deeper wisdom. This process takes intentional work. Deeper wisdom is spiritual and is buried in sacred text, and it requires a balance of our hearts and will to breech a higher understanding of knowledge.

As I neared the end of my time in Fort Myers, I said my goodbyes to the school and all the new friendships that I had made. The time seem to go by so fast. It was a painful and emotional departure, especially with the few I had developed a special closeness with. Saying goodbye to my boss at my night job was especially difficult. She was more than a boss. We built a wonderful friendship. She provided me with a feeling of love and a place to call home. She listened to all my concerns and offered me grace during my immaturity. She provided me with a connection and a place to call home for the two years I was in college. This relationship was the most difficult to say goodbye. She had become my best friend, mentor, and supporter.

As I pulled out of the gas station, the tears began to stream down my cheeks. All I remember is playing the only cassette that I owned, by Waylon Jennings, as I selected the repeat mode as I drove out of town. My departure was difficult, but I knew that I must return home to continue my four-year degree at my local university. This transition is just one example of many that we will experience in our lives. It is important to check in with the soul's discernment as we negotiate these passageways. Choosing the soul's path will provide higher opportunities for the soul to evolve and grow. The soul plans various transformational experiences to help it evolve to a new, higher aspect.

When I returned home, I moved in with my twin sister and began the enrollment process for school. I don't remember the details, but I did try out for the university softball team and made it. Nevertheless,

I was selected as a walk-on without a scholarship. I was disappointed with this outcome, but somehow it wasn't as meaningful as my experience down south.

I managed to play softball for the local four-year university for about a year but decided not to pursue a position my senior year. I just did not connect with the new team. I didn't really feel a bond with any of the players. I didn't really know any of them on a personal level. The campus was so large that we hardly saw each other in class or at other common places.

The lack of a scholarship caused me to seek employment to help pay for books and living expenses. I got two part-time jobs! I worked for an afternoon day care facility and a communications company during my senior year in college. These two years were both difficult and fun. I still struggled academically and wasn't sure if I would ever become comfortable in any academic setting. I did manage to meet new friends in a community league softball program as well. These new friends would offer me a place to stay for my last year in college and we became a family. Once again, I was struggling this time in algebra and one of my roommates happen to major in math. Nothing happens by chance. There are people all over the place to help us as we negotiate this journey. At this point, I could not see where I would end up in ten years, but I at least knew that I was to complete my bachelor's of sports science. We are not given a view of our entire life. We are given segments to live out as a way of learning and growing. There would be no opportunities for growth if we already knew the complete plan.

This segment of my life finally came to a close as I was approved for graduation the winter of 1984.

CHAPTER TWO

Army Highlights

We move in cycles in our lives. My graduation was merely a bridge that led me to my next soul experience in life. Considering my bachelor's degree was in sports science education, I tried to secure a job that matched this experience so I interviewed for a physical education vacancy. This position happened to be in the same school where I was completing my teaching requirements. I just knew that I would get the job. It just so happened that my internship was nearing completion and I could transition right into this new position. I did apply and interview for the position; however, the school principal chose someone else for the position. I was crushed. At the time, it seemed to all line up. When I inquired with the principal as to why I wasn't selected, his simple answer was that I lacked experience.

What I saw then as a missed opportunity was in fact destiny. If I was meant to have the physical education position, I would have gotten the job. Life is easier to understand looking backward. Not securing the physical education position caused me to seek the military as a possible avenue for my future. My stepdad had been talking with me and encouraged me to apply. This path both challenged me and intrigued me. I wanted an opportunity to learn electronics and knew that military training would be stellar on a resume. I chose to go army because they guaranteed me a specific job class. I felt that job opportunities and pay would be higher in the electronics field once I got out.

This move was a bold and scary move for me. I was uneasy. In one sense, I was afraid of the extreme negative environment and people yelling at me. On the other hand, I valued the electronics training and the experience more than my fear. I knew military experience would be beneficial and open many doors.

I never planned to stay for retirement. I just knew military retirement was not my path. However, I did enroll full time for a four-year commitment and an additional two-year conditional stay.

Every major decision impacts life's future. The decision to join the military still impacts me to this day. Because I didn't let fear stand in the way, I am now a veteran and still benefiting from this experience. I joined the army in the winter of 1986 in the delayed entry program but left for basic training to Anniston, Alabama, in February 1987.

The environment just as I suspected was brutal. Drill sergeants yelling at me and the mind games really took a toll on me mentally and emotionally. But again, these experiences help to make us who we are today. These uncomfortable moments force us to grow and I grew physically, emotionally, and mentally. In the beginning, I questioned myself as to why I signed up for the army; the experience made me a stronger person.

After completing over two months of basic training, I was sent to Fort Eustis logistics school for my primary helicopter electronic training. I was actually learning what I wanted to learn: electronics. I'm laughing out loud now, but at the time, I didn't realize the electronics training was weaponry armament in the field. The recruiters failed to stress this part. The video clip showed people working on the bench. This is a naive lesson in making sure one understands specific job details before agreeing to sign on the dotted line. After Advance Individual Training (AIT), I was assigned to K Company, 159th, Hunter Army Airfield in Savannah, Georgia. Once there, I eventually cross-trained as a 68 N, which meant that I was responsible for maintaining and troubleshooting electrical issues with the navigational systems on board helicopters, which I enjoyed.

However, during my first few months at Hunter Army Airfield, I spent one week in the field loading TOW (tube-launched optically tracked wired) guided missiles on Cobra helicopters. It was at this point that I learned that the recruiter failed to reveal the entire job duties. I learned in a most uncomfortable way that my original MOS, a 68J, was a field technician who was responsible for loading and repairing electronic weaponry systems on board various helicopters. Thankfully, the universe corrected a vibrational change, and I was cross-trained as a 68 N, which was a repairer of navigational electronics on board helicopters. This work I enjoyed and excelled at. The time I spent on the flight line provided breathtaking opportunities to immerse myself in just being one with God. I witnessed many breathtaking sunrises and sunsets. These times offered me some contemplation time and meditative moments that helped me connect with source. I really don't think I understood my soul's needs during this time, but I could feel the solace and calming effects that these moments provided spiritually when I took the time to get out of the material life.

Like most of us, I was caught in life's work loop. Working ten hours a day and always returning to work the next day became a repetitious form of insanity. I still longed for some type of connection. I wasn't really connecting with my army peers. I needed some meaningful relationships. Something deeper. So I leaned back into my softball passion to help me meet and develop meaningful relationships. This would be a huge turning point in my life.

Falling in Love

I signed up for a community coed and women's softball league. This was just what I needed. New friends that I could get to know and develop meaningful relationships. A place not connected to the base where I could be myself and get to know new friends. It is our friends in our lives who help us through our many challenges. I went to the ball fields and looked for an opportunity to be pickup on a team. Many times these teams keep seasoned players who play every year so I had to find someone willing to give an outsider a chance. I tried out for a particular team and was accepted. It took me a while to get to know everyone on the team, but I soon developed the friendships that I had hoped for.

This particular team participated in the women's league and in a coed league in the fall. This particular year, I was unable to play in the fall coed league. I was scheduled for some advance army training in Fort Eustis, Virginia. The training would only last a few months, and I would return. Nevertheless, they had to look for another player to meet the requirements for the coed team. This is when life got complicated for me. The person who filled in for me during the winter was also asked to play on our women's league the following year and she accepted. As I returned to the women's softball league, I was introduced to this new person. The more time I spent with her, the more we connected. It was a connection that I had never developed before. The longer we played softball together, the more we got to know each other both on and off the softball field.

This relationship was a unique one I had never experienced. We would talk for hours, usually around life topics. I remember speaking often about God topics. During this time, I was still shaped in my old religious beliefs around my Catholic teachings that really sent me reeling because I knew that I had fallen in love with her. I was afraid of the "hellfire" damnation religiosity that I was taught around same sex relationships. At work, I kept repeating, "How can something that feels so right be so wrong?" Of course, I absolutely had no one to talk with. This topic was very new to me. I had met gay people before but was never face-to-face with a paradoxical event that had the potential to help me discover my true identity.

This was before the "Don't ask. Don't tell" policy. The military had a history of investigating these kinds of events and dishonorably discharging people. I was too close to the end of my service, and I certainly did not want it to end like that. This was a pivotal moment in my life. I had two choices: to embrace my true sexual identity as a lesbian or deny my core identity and live a lie. For years, I tried to fit into the heterosexual lifestyle that was the mainstream binary culture at the time. Choosing not to be the person that God created me to be just did not seem to be an option.

These are moments that really define who we are at our core. We can choose the simple path and acquiesce to the norms of society, or we can follow our inner compasses and let our souls lead us to self-identity. Self-identity is critical to living an authentic life. Our self-identity and sexuality are at the intersection of spirituality. These two cannot be separated. Living into our true self liberates not only our souls but also stretches our understanding of who God or the divine really is. God is so much more than the limitations that people and institutions define. The Creator loves the creation or the creation would not exist. God cannot hate the masterpiece if we believe that God is love. The two cannot coexist.

I could run from these wonderful authentic feelings of love or deny my true authentic self. Embracing my sexuality as a lesbian introduced me to a more loving God. My Catholic faith inculcated a more punitive God. A God who judged and condemned humanity for falling short. Ironically, by embracing the unknown path, it eventually led me to a more loving and accepting God.

My choice to pursue my new relationship actually motivated me to begin my own spiritual journey concerning truths about God. I no longer could rely on someone else's understanding for my soul's salvation. It forced me to look for other explanations to reconcile my new love with God. I was suddenly emerged in a new life full of life, love, and deep connection, but it would still take me quite some time to reconcile my same sex relationship with God. My new friends seemed to have an inner knowing that God loved them and that was enough, but for me, I had to need a deeper understanding of this acceptance.

My exposure to the lesbian world allowed me to see a different spectrum around sexual expression. Love is love, as the expression goes, and this is so true. We can't pick and choose who God loves. God's expression of love is unlimited. People's ideas about what is right or what is wrong are very limited because of religious misunderstandings. How can there only be one way to express God's love? Is God only in heterosexual relationships? Of course not. If anything, I have learned that we shape our understandings of right and wrong based on the biases of our parents, grandparents, and religious understanding of what we assume is acceptable. I would have never understood this if I had been too afraid to explore my sexuality. If I had stayed with the traditional understandings of social norms, I never would have found myself or God for that matter. Following my inner knowing opened me up to a whole new world of various beliefs and understandings about life's possibilities.

I was in the last six months of my army enlistment obligation when I fell in love in June 1990. I had accrued sixty days of leave and planned to leave the army on December 24, 1990. I saw this as my Christmas present to myself. However, this plan didn't quite work out. On August 7, 1990, the United States organized Operation Desert Shield, which became Operation Desert Storm, and the army froze all military personnel's ability to exit the service. This news was horrendous for me. I had just fallen in love, and now I had to leave for Saudi Arabia for a period of time the government was calling "indefinite." I had all kinds of mixed emotions going on. I was scared not knowing if I would ever come back to the States and was grieving the absence of a new relationship that had just developed but was suddenly put on hold.

Coming Out

I was actually home on leave when I received word that our company had been deployed. I came home to have a private conversation with my mother about my new same-sex relationship and to explain to her that I had fallen in love. Many LGBTQ+ people are faced with making a decision to come out to their family and loved ones. This is not an easy task. It takes courage. My biggest fear was that my mom would be disappointed that there would be no traditional wedding and a high probability of no grandchildren. I didn't want to disappoint her. She was my main concern at the time. I wanted or needed her to understand. How could she though? There were very few LGBTQ+ people living an outted life. During that time, the LGBTQ+ people hid their private lives for fear of losing their army careers. They were also concerned for their health, safety, and lives. It was a difficult conversation, but ultimately, she said that she wanted me to be happy.

My leave ended, and I returned to Savannah. There were no promises of me coming back alive from the Middle East, so I had to prepare life's essentials before I left. I needed to know that things would be handled in case I never made it back. I turned my financial responsibility over to my partner. She would manage making my car payment, the phone bill, and any other kinds of bills. I also had to make sure that my family knew what my final wishes were for my belongings so I made a phone call to my dad. I explained that I had been deployed and that if anything happened to me that my partner was entitled to my physical belongings at the apartment we shared. I also explained that my financial things were already taken care of. He wasn't too receptive to this information; he felt like his role was being "usurped." To me it made perfect sense and what anyone else would have done in any other type of relationship.

Now that my last wishes were made known to my family, I had to prepare myself for deployment. Because I thought that I was getting out of the army, I only owned one uniform and needed to purchase several pairs before I left for deployment. The army happened to order tan desert fatigues for our deployment and I was given two sets of these, which helped. I bought other necessary items, such as T-shirts and socks. I had no idea what to expect once I deployed. We were also issued tan desert boots that were more comfortable than the black ones we were issued. My partner and I tried to make the best of the situation. We embraced every last minute we had with one another. Those last memories would be what I would take with me to Saudi and live on until I returned home, hopefully.

The army finally locked us down on Hunter Army Air Base, Savannah, Georgia, and we were not allowed to leave a secure, fenced compound. My partner did come and visit me through a fence, but it was too much for me to see her and not be able to embrace her so I asked her to leave. Asking her to leave was the hardest thing that I ever had to do. It wasn't that I wanted her to leave. I loved her more than life itself, but I could not bear to feel the pain and grief welling up inside me, knowing that I was about to leave the love of my life.

Falling in love with her was the catalyst that helped me understand my true identity. Our love forced me to search the depths of my soul to try to figure out who I was at soul level. I remember asking myself, "How can something that feels so right can be so wrong?" Of course, this belief was an incorrect impression from my Catholic roots.

Catholicism taught me that God punishes people for not obeying God's laws. My family roots of Catholicism provided me with zero answers, and it only recited man-made doctrine that obscured the truth. It only conjured confusion and fear within me. It would be much later in life that I learned that God is love, and if God is love, God can't be anything outside love. More on this later.

As I stood inside the secure, fenced compound, I felt so lost and so isolated to life. I was leaving the only person who truly knew and understood me. She was the only person I connected with on a soul level. I knew that I was leaving an irreplaceable bond that would be impossible to fill as I deployed to Saudi. It would be impossible to speak about our relationship as the army disapproved.

It was painful seeing her on the other side of the fence that separated us. After requesting her to leave, I regretted it. My stomach was in knots. I already missed her terribly, but I tried to focus my attention on loading cattle trucks and airplanes with duffle bags and equipment as our unit preceded to load many other units for their takeoff.

After three or four weeks of loading other units for deployment, it was finally our time to load ourselves. On the last day, we loaded on a C-5. I was in disbelief that I was actually headed overseas to a war of all places. My fear was dying in a strange, war-torn country and never seeing my loved ones again. As we loaded the C-5, we were guided upstairs from the cargo area to the sitting area in the upper level. I can still hear my M-16 rifle clanging on the steel stairs leading to the upper sitting deck. The steps to the cabin area were so steep and I was so short that my M-16 rifle clanked on the metal steps as I navigated upstairs. The cabin area was not like an ordinary plane. The seats were backward, and of course there were no flight attendants to serve a complimentary drink and meal. However, we were issued military meals ready to eat (MREs). Of course this just solidified the reality of our deployment.

Desert Storm

We landed on Dhahran airfield in late August 1990. My arrival was surreal. I was in shock. Not only did I find myself in a war, but I was approximately eight thousand miles from home. I was accustomed to hot summers in the South, but the temperature in Saudi was around 125 degrees. The desert air was very dry without a breeze to generate cross-air circulation. The air was stagnate and thick and hovered close to our dirty bodies. Dhahran airfield was only an initial landing pad. It lacked hygiene accommodations of running water, showers, and plumbed toilets.

We camped on Dhahran airfield in open army tents during the night, and during the day, we worked from our shelter portable expandable aircraft maintenance shops (SPAM units). These containers held our electronic equipment for testing aircraft components and other navigational aircraft systems.

We camped on Dhahran airfield for two weeks before receiving orders to move to an unknown area in the desert. As we convoyed to our next site, I had no way of knowing exactly where we were; however, as we exited the highway, I did see a sign that read "Desert Access." This would become our first military strategic camping site for what would be a long four months.

I cannot express the shock of having to live outside in such primitive conditions. The desert landscape was primeval and desolate. As we were setting up our tents, a horrendous sandstorm blew across the desert, making vision impossible. I had never witnessed such a powerful and incapacitating sandstorm. Hurricanes yes, but not sandstorms. It was impossible to continue setting up our tents. The sand grit stung as it brushed across our face and skin. We could not see beyond an arm's length, and sand grit found its way into our eyes, clothes, hair, and any open orifices. We were immobilized because of a lack of sight. We were issued eye goggles, but they were insufficient.

Nevertheless, we had to press on because we needed shelter for the night. I experienced disbelief, grief, and culture shock as I desperately tried to adjust to the rugged desert conditions. We saw our first iguana as we were assembling Bedouin tents during our first camp night. The first few months were very difficult. I was lost, lonely, and afraid that this war would either take my life or—even worse—last a long time. As I had feared, I was alone and had no one to talk to openly about my grief and relationship. Initially, there was no one that I was willing to trust and open up to regarding my same-sex relationship. The military was and still is steeped in an oppressive belief system that understands queer relationships are immoral.

These beliefs are a result of erroneous influences from toxic generational programing around what is understood as acceptable ethics, moral beliefs, and religious dogma. These foundational infrastructures influence social and gender norms. It would have been a gamble for me to open up to just anyone who might report it, jeopardizing retaliatory consequences from individuals and the command. I wasn't willing to take the risk. I felt isolated and invisible as a lesbian. In *Sexuality and the Sacred*, Marvin Ellis and Kelly Brown Douglas write, "Sexuality is about the overall potential for human relationships." Simply, we connect and build relationships with individuals who share commonality with our sexuality and gender identity. There are other factors that are important when building relationships, such as trust, understanding, and openness. Sexuality is a crucial aspect of one's beingness. It determines how we do things, and it shapes our thoughts and feelings.

During my time in the military, there was much divisiveness and hostility around any type of sexuality outside heteronormative. There was also an absence of inclusive and diverse language that embraced queer sexuality. The lack of inclusive language and education around diverse human sexuality contributed to hostile conversations, oppression, and judgment around queer sexuality. Our connection with others helps to ground us. Grounding helps us feel more secure, stable, and balanced with ourselves and Mother Earth. Retrospectively, I understand now that my feelings of detachment, grief, and fear were the reason that I began seeking spiritual answers about my soul's journey and purpose.

My horrendous experience in Saudi's desert forced me to get out of my physical self and look for deeper answers and meaning elsewhere. The only place that I knew to begin looking was the limited God that I was introduced to in my formative years. My initial fear immobilized me, and I knew that I needed something greater to hold onto if I was going to survive this war experience. By the way, the iguana that I saw the night we were setting up camp has some wise insight to my desert experience. One resource suggested that the Iguana's message to us that night was to "lie low until a threat passes or to be flexible and adaptable to change." The iguana's symbolism also reminds us that we should be joyful in all situations (www.spirit-animals.com). If I had realized this that night, it might have given me some insight or at the very least some contemplative wisdom for reflection.

We are all born into this physical plane called earth. We are dense beings who have forgotten that we are spiritual beings having physical experiences. Our egos run our lives through fear until we are able to separate the "Christ consciousness" from ego. This requires that we awaken the power that sits at the base of our spines.

It takes many lives for most of us to raise our conscious awareness high enough to awaken our souls. However, my experience in Saudi's desert would prove to be a beginning to this higher path.

All spiritual journeys evolve as they unfold. In this initial stage of my spiritual path, I had limited knowledge of that spiritual process. My only recourse was to reconnect with my childhood religion. This God was anthropomorphic, male, white, and lived in heaven. This move would spark an inward contemplation and become the beginning of my spiritual journey in seeking answers and life purpose. At the time, I wasn't aware of how much influence this war would impact my mental and emotional well-being. Traumatic events can become trapped in our bodies, and when we do not heal these energetically, they can cause imbalances and diseases and make us sick. It would take most of my adult life to learn how to heal and balance my energetic bodies. It would also take most of my life to redefine who God was for me. This was part of the journey.

My company was a support regiment that maintained electronics on helicopters, and there were few women. It was difficult working in an environment so male dominated. It was hard living and working in close confines twenty-four/seven with people I did not personally know. Because of my sexuality and gender, I led a private and personal life off base. Somehow this war invaded the privacy of my most intimate revelations. I found myself working and living with people I preferred to keep at a distance.

This war forced me to interact with people I normally would not have interacted with. In order to survive the Saudi deployment, I would need to stretch out of my comfort zone and begin to develop some sort of support system, even if the relationships looked and felt different. Some side of me needed to connect with people on a deeper level. At the time, I wasn't even sure what this meant, but I knew it was missing. I needed to feel connected and grounded to the present moment if I was going to make it through this conflict. Grounding is necessary! It helps us to feel alive and gives us hope that things will get better. When we feel alone, aloof, and grieving, it is impossible for our souls to feel connected to life conditions.

I had to come to terms and grips with the present reality that I was not going home anytime soon. This was a scary thought. The command informed us that we were assigned "indefinitely" to this ancient and undeveloped desert along with its patriarchal society. It was a phrase that echoed fear in every cell of my body and left no room for hope. This information traumatized me in many ways. It was disturbing to think that I was trapped in a foreign, desolate land with strangers I didn't even know. It was disturbing in so many ways.

This experience certainly helped me to understand why people feel hopeless in times of deep angst, believing that things will never get better. This is why we must get out of ourselves and try hard to focus on higher thought vibrations. What we think we become. My mental, spiritual, and emotional health needed to feel connected with souls who were more evolved, more loving, and more aware. If you are in this situation, try to believe that things will get better, and trust the guidance of your soul and guides. These calamities have a way of awakening us to our true authentic self and purpose. Hold on until you can experience a shift that will springboard you to the other side, where an oasis is waiting for your transformed self.

The only comfort that I found while I was in Saudi's primitive desert was when I worked the flight line where I maintained the navigational systems onboard the helicopters. I worked on the flight line with two people who became my brothers. They were my support while I was deployed. We saw each other every day! We were like family. Thank God for these brothers as they helped me to cope with the deployment. For my birthday, one of them drew a birthday card, and they all signed it. Like most brothers, they were not very affectionate, but in that moment, I felt their love for me. And it bonded me to them on a soul level. This helped me to feel that I was a part of a tribe so to speak, the "flight line" tribe.

I would spend my birthday, Thanksgiving, and Christmas in the Saudi desert. My mom was of course upset and worried about my well-being. She feared the worse. Dad stayed abreast of the news and tried to stay informed about the deployment details. The last few months of 1990 seemed to creep along. I was homesick and grieving being away from the love of my life and my family. One thing that kept me going was mail call. I received a letter every day from my partner. Letter turnaround was about thirty days; however, once we began writing, we tried to write each other every day. This really did help me. My family also wrote me, and my mom sent cookies. My twin sister would also write letters before her workday. This contact lifted my spirits and gave me hope that this war would end soon. I spent many days on the flight line watching the sun rise and set as I wrote letters and talked to God. I could not understand why I had to go through all this pain. I saw no point in any it of it.

Of course, life is really lived forward and understood backward. This experience would shake me to my core. It would begin to stir a spiritual aspect in me. The soul grows in uncomfortable times and situations. It is the soul's hope or our higher self's aspiration to ascend spiritually while here in physical form. At the time, I did not have any concept or understanding about the workings of the soul. My fear and anxiety caused me to begin spending more time with God and the universe. This experience caused me to seek answers and support inwardly. I sought answers, understanding, and comfort as I read scripture and sat with God's wonders in the middle of the desert.

I didn't realize it at the time, but I started to practice embracing the present moment. I began to embody God's beautiful universe, the sunrises, the sunsets, the stars, the moon, and the constellations. I had never before witnessed such magnificent sunrises and sunsets. Saudi's desert offered me an intimate seat where I could witness the Creator's most spectacular and majestic creation in the awesome skyline. This experience always reminded me that there was something greater beyond my current time, space, and awareness. These wonders would help me to connect with my partner eight thousand miles away. I began to realize that the majestic skyline that I was observing was the same skyline that she was seeing. The desert terrain reminded me of times that my family and I spent on the beaches. We drove dune buggies while negotiating sand cliffs as we played in the Creator's beautiful landscape.

Our family spent time camping, fishing, and soaking up the sun's rays as we explored the sugar-white sand beaches of my hometown. Saudi's desert sunrises, sunsets, and starry night sky offered me a time to reflect and sit in oneness with the universe. In this oneness, I held all my loved ones ever so close and contemplated my return home.

The old saying that absence makes the heart grow fonder is so true. I missed those I loved. My heart went out, especially to my mother, who was worried for her daughter's well-being. She wrote me when she was able. It was inspirational and uplifting to begin my day on the flight line watching the sun come up in Saudi's desert as I responded to letters back home. I spent this time nurturing my soul and refueling spiritually. The letters provided hope for a near future when I was able to physically reconnect with all my loved ones when I returned to the States.

I received letters from home, and they would become my tether to those dear and close to me in the States. Nothing like a desert experience to realize that we are relational people and need relationships to thrive. We need opportunities to express love in our everyday lives. It is love that develops and awakens the soul to its higher self. We are all divine, but we have forgotten our true nature of divinity.

Back then, I knew nothing about meditation and its benefits to my overall health. Nevertheless, somehow my inner self knew exactly what it needed, and thankfully, I responded by making myself available to stillness on the flight line frequently. This self-reflection time provided me with much calmness and peace. This experience provided me with a greater connection to the cosmos and the divine. This connection offered me with spiritual nourishment as it connected me to Mother Gaia, which grounded me and helped me feel safe, secure, and hopeful. We would spend Thanksgiving and Christmas in our "desert access" location. I will admit spending holidays in the desert was very difficult to get through. Holidays are very special to me as I use this time to connect with family. While in the States, my partner and I traveled home to spend a few days connecting with my family during the holiday seasons. Christmas is my mom's favorite time of the year, and she always looked forward to spending time with her children during this time.

In late December or early January, we moved north to a new camp near Kuwait border and set up again. We made phone calls the night before January 17, 1991, and learned that Desert Storm had been declared. We remained in war with Iraq for a total of forty-three days, ending on my mom's birthday: February 28. Although the war was over, it would still take another two months for our unit to be deployed back home. We continued daily aircraft flight operations and repairs, but we would also begin a massive decontamination and cleaning process that included every piece of equipment that we owned. This process would include a microscopic cleaning of every maintenance item that was assigned to us. Our entire unit had to clean every tool, aircraft, SPAM unit, and other assigned items. These items would be inspected from the Department of Customs before allowing us to cross international borders. This stage of deployment uplifted me, knowing that soon I would be heading home to my loved ones. The decontamination process kept me busy and hopeful while knowing that I would soon be home.

Coming Home

I will never forget the commercial flight that flew us home from Saudi. There was so much excitement in the air. Everyone was thrilled to be going home. I called my partner and gave her all the details of my arrival. I also made a phone call to my mother and father. With this news, they all planned a trip to Savannah to celebrate my return. My parents, grandparents, twin sister, and an aunt came up from Florida to greet me. This would be a very special day! The return flight home would take approximately twenty hours. There was such jubilee on the commercial flight home that nobody slept. We were scheduled for a layover in Bangor, Maine, then continued to Hunter Army Airfield, Savannah, Georgia, on April 14,1991.

I remember when we touched down in Bangor, Maine. As I made my way to the payphones, people were celebrating our return. People were giving us all kinds of things, such as flowers, ribbons, and drinks, and some wanted autographs. As I worked my way to the phone booth, I noticed a TV crew following me. I couldn't believe my eyes when they started filming me as I approached the phones and dialed my number. I was in awe and surprised that this many people arrived to show gratitude for our service in Saudi. It was an awe-inspiring moment.

I dialed my partner but had to leave my arrival details on our answering machine. Our layover in Bangor was quick, and we were off in the skies again en route to Hunter Army Airfield, Savannah, Georgia. Our destination would be the very point where I had departed over seven months ago. It was surreal!

My arrival was complex and caused some anxiety for my partner and parents. They had never met each other in person. My partner prepared as best as she could not only for my return from Saudi but also for the many guests who would arrive later at our house. It wasn't the best conditions for meeting my parents. She didn't just meet one parent that day; she also met my father, paternal grandfather, one aunt, and of course, my mother. She had already met my twin sister earlier in the year, and that introduction was strained as my sister did not approve of our relationship.

Although it was the happiest day of my life, I had no idea how my family was going to react to my partner. As I landed, I could see a banner with my name on it—held by my partner and sister. The celebrations on the flight line were joyous; everyone was elated to see me. My mom was so excited to see me that she yelled my name across the flight line when she saw me get off the plane. I had never seen her so happy. I am sure she was thanking God that I had made it home safely.

It was wonderful being back in the United States. I had learned to appreciate my freedom not only as a citizen but as a woman. As I continued the debriefing process, I was ushered to a secured area where I turned in my M-16 rifle. My separation from it was a relief. As I continued, I was briefly reunited with my partner, and we made our way back to the rest of my family as they awaited my arrival. My dad seemed to glow as he gave me a hug, and to my surprise, my grandfather and aunt were also there to see me home. I was on cloud nine.

We all left the base in our different cars and met at our house to continue the celebrations. The situation was awkward as my two lives suddenly converged in our living room. Thankfully, before my deployment, I had already"come out to my parents. It was a very difficult thing to do, but I knew that I had to finalize things just in case something happened to me while I was deployed to Saudi. I still remember the conversation with my mom in what would be the last face-to-face conversation before I deployed. She did not necessarily understand it, but I do remember her telling me that all she wanted was for me to be happy. We expressed our love for one another, and from that point forward, we both moved on.

As we sat in our living room celebrating my return from Saudi, we all tried to ignore the preverbal elephant in the room. I could feel the discomfort with those present. We mainly discussed the experiences that I was willing to share from Saudi and left the obvious topic for a later discussion.

CHAPTER THREE

Returning to Civilian Life

When I returned to Savannah, Georgia, from Saudi, Arabia, I was invited to reenlist, but I declined. From the onset of my enlistment, I never felt the desire to make a career out of the army. I just knew that I should continue following my soul's guidance. The army always seemed so uncomfortable for me. I never felt like I fit. I always felt isolated and all alone. Even when I was surrounded by an entire unit of people in uniform. I found friendship in those I connected with on a deeper level. There were many times over the course of my enlistment that I felt as if I had made the wrong decision to enlist. However, I am reminded that there are no coincidences. The military infrastructure and those who governed the day-to-day operations seemed so far removed from caring about those who they led. For me, the organization never seemed to promote or show any concern or compassion for the souls they led. Like religion, it was missing the feminine aspect qualities of love, compassion, intuition, and other feminine gifts.

In the nineties and somewhat still today, the military understands the world through a patriarchal and heteronormative view. This means that many objectified women. The military has a history of sexual assaults that violated women's bodies, and they refused to hold perpetuators accountable. Many of these cases were dismissed as "boys being boys."

These beliefs were shaped by family, social norms, and religious beliefs. In addition, commercials, television, movies, and other educational platforms affirm these oppressive beliefs. These infrastructures are fractured and have required centuries of justice work to deconstruct. Meanwhile, women continue to be oppressed, violated, injured, and valued less than their male counterparts. With the recent "Me Too" movement and other movements like it, we are slowly changing the way people see gender roles and identity. As I say this, I do want to recognize the progress we have made in the last century in dismantling misogyny and other inequalities around justice issues. Many light workers have come in at this time to dismantle these harmful belief structures and to make a way forward to the new golden age that leads with equality, love, wisdom, and respect for people and their bodies.

In healthy partnerships, the masculine and feminine energy work in tangent with one another to accomplish enlightenment, oneness, or universal consciousness. A balanced alignment with both the masculine and feminine energies is required for the soul's ascension. The masculine energy is the (active) energy. Active energy is required to get us moving. It motivates us. It also helps us reason things out. The feminine energy is the (creative) energy, and it offers love, compassion, and intuition. It moves in swirls, while the masculine energy moves with a direct, logical order. These two energies work in tangent to become equal cocreators with God. These two energies push and pull as they dance together, creating beauty in the material world.

As I have said before, the soul comes here to earth to balance, learn, and realign its energy. It is very beneficial for the soul's growth when we step out of ego to identify and then work to heal our shadow issues. It is easy for the ego to claim that the personality has everything under control, but this is far from the truth. The ego doesn't want any correction. It likes the current arrangement with the personality. To clarify, the personality has a tendency to believe the fear that the ego is whispering, such as "I am not good enough," "I am not smart enough," "I am shameful," and "I am a loser." These are all lies. These are beliefs that are trapped in the memories of our cells. To break this cycle, we must believe that we are divine and powerful. If we believe that we are created from source/God, then we must be powerful. The soul comes here to encounter experiences. These experiences are not labeled "good" or "bad." This would be judgment. Judgment creates separation, and there is no separation. God or the divine is within each of us and does not judge.

I cannot stress the importance of purging our bodies of past negative karma. Pay attention to synchronicities, and the universe will reveal our shadow work. For me, the universe was calling me to balance both my masculine and feminine energies. Before my awakening, I had no idea that I was neglecting a vital aspect of my spiritual embodiment. Spirit showed me how important it was to balance and heal my energies. My awakening revealed to me that if I was going to accomplish a spiritual union in this lifetime, I desperately needed to heal past injuries as a result of the wounded masculine energy and other hurtful experiences. Spirit taught me the importance of living from the heart. We must learn to forgive and love for our own soul growth. Refusing to do this holds our souls captive to this 3D space and the cycles of life.

We come here to become something *greater* than our human egos, human limitations, and human tragedies. Each of us arrives here with a purpose and lesson in mind. Remember this is a spiritual journey. We are here to recall that divine aspect that already exists within us. We just have to figure out how to rediscover it and then adjust our compass setting to follow the new sacred compass bearing.

Once we are in alignment to our divine aspect, we can begin to pull from our sacred spiritual power.

This spiritual power opens a divine aspect of us that we are unaware of. An unawakened soul subconsciously believes that it is a victim to its past mistakes and painful experiences. It also believes that it is the sole source of knowledge. This toxic program begins to undermine our hope and aspiration to be something greater.

These inconsistencies can be difficult to identify and correct before the soul is awakened. It is a process. Remember in Christian scripture Saul killed the new Christians. He believed he was doing right. This thinking was a result of his personal ego, personal will, and old pharisaic beliefs. After his awakening, Saul's new name was Paul—the apostle Paul. A new person, a new birth, a spiritual birth! Paul suddenly had awakened to his divine self. I point out all this to say that we must tap into our sacred power so that it can save us from our egos. We must surrender to the divine. It knows the way home.

Returning To Civilian Life

I had no idea what I wanted to do when I returned home from Saudi so I took extended leave with the military. I used this paid time off to rest and spend time with my partner. The extended leave also allowed me time to readjust to civilian life, and at some point, I would need to begin looking for employment.

There were plenty of things that needed reacclimatizing. For one, I had to relearn how to navigate around town. It is amazing how spending seven months in the desert will mess with your mind and memory. I had to relearn to do the simplest things like write checks, drive a car, and accomplish other life skills. This time would serve as a transition into the next phase of my life. As the weeks passed, it was soon time to actively seek civilian employment.

Fortunately, I was able to land a job at Lockheed Martin. I couldn't have asked for a better transitional job. Ironically, the job involved disassembling and reassembling the Apache Attack Helicopter (AH-64). These aircrafts were returning home from Saudi Arabia and desperately needed a functional and structural overhaul. This overhaul would include every system on the aircraft. Some of these systems renovated included electrical, avionics, sheet metal, mechanical, and more. As these systems were dismantled, a rigorous cleaning routine of the aircraft was performed. This process was critical in restoring the aircraft to optimal performance. The rigorous cleaning removed desert sand and debris that was slowly deteriorating the aircraft's mainframe, blades, electrical components, and electrical terminal boards. My job as an electrician was to deconstruct electrical systems and clean and then reinstall the various electrical components to include avionics, controls, instruments, and navigation. Once these individual systems were reinstalled, power-on checks were performed, and then the various systems were ready for a collective flight readiness check. This test integrated all systems to ensure they were communicating properly and sending appropriate signals. Finally, a flight readiness test was scheduled for a test pilot to perform an in-air systems check. Once these passed, the AH-64 helicopters were returned to their assigned companies. My daily tasks at Lockheed were very similar to my predeployment work life. I say it was a wonderful transitional job because it allowed me to transition to civilian life while still doing something that I already knew. The transition was perfect. My work location moved one hangar north on Hunter Army Airfield flight line. It was strange returning and working on the same flight line that I flew out of a year earlier to Saudi Arabia. This time, I was more appreciative of life and the once overlooked things, such as a secure surrounding, a secure job, and a wonderful support system to include a loving partner, friends, and family.

As a result of Desert Storm, my partner and I formed a close relationship with God. Our letters centered on God, and this provided us with faith and strength for my hopeful return home. In my absence, she was attending a loving church and was baptized. Later she transferred to a new church and began to immerse herself in learning and teaching scripture. We continued our spiritual studies when I returned from Desert Storm. She led a disciple Bible study program and we spent time researching and discussing God, Jesus, and scripture together. This was a new embarkment for both of us. I was raised Catholic and never really had an opportunity to study scripture. Studying scripture helped us to stay focused on God as we continued to strengthen our spiritual awareness. The more we centered God in our lives, the more we connected on a spiritual level. I guess when one experiences a traumatic event such as Desert Storm, one realizes just how much life is a gift.

I had been working for Lockheed for about a year when a modification and repair job opportunity was presented to me. This position would require travel and installing wiring for the transmission rotor chip detector for the Huey Helicopter (UH-1). I certainly did not want to be on the road again away from my partner, but the salary was hard to ignore. The plan was to do this for a year and hopefully return with a more secured financial situation. I actually only committed to doing this for about six months, but the team foreman talked me into finishing the contract. It was a profitable experience, and it would benefit a future job in aviation electronics.

Even in my new position as an electrician with Lockheed, I continued living a closeted life while at work. I refrained from discussing anything personal, and I certainly did not share my most treasured relationship while I was at work. Although my uniform changed, the environment was identical to my military experience. Most of the flight line and support personnel were prior military and heterosexual. Most of these people retired from the military and were working their second jobs to secure retirement. Once again, I was in the minority. The traveling modification team at least offered me a break from the ordinary flight line crass attitudes and foul conversations. The modification team consisted of three people: a foreman lead, a mechanic, and of course me as the electrician. This team was very mature and easy to work with. I respected both individuals, and we developed a tight bond. These relationships were meaningful and authentic. We need authentic relationships in our lives to thrive and feel connected.

Atlanta

The UH-1 "chip detector" modification contract ended sometime around August 1993, and this presented yet another transition. This transition would require a physical move. My partner's father's health was declining, and we made the decision to move to Atlanta, Georgia, so that she could be closer to her parents to allow for more visitation and to provide support when needed. This transition was uncertain, and the way forward seemed foggy and unclear in the beginning.

I grew up in a small town and was uncomfortable with the challenges of negotiating such a large city. The intergraded interstate highways in Atlanta challenged my lack of navigational skills. Instead of taking twenty minutes to get across town, I had to plan for an hour or more. Having to learn my way around contributed to my uneasiness. There is something about the familiarity of our surroundings. It somehow provides awareness and grounding for our physical, spiritual, and psychological security. It is one thing to be lost in your hometown but quite another to be lost in a metropolis.

Learning how to navigate was just one facet of this transition that needed proficiency. The next thing that I needed to accomplish was gaining some sort of direction or goal around my vocation. What would I do for employment? I enjoyed working on helicopters while I was in the military. I felt comfortable, and it seemed to be a perfect fit. I enjoyed the challenge of troubleshooting the cause of an electronic issue and then repairing it. I had purposely chosen electronics as my military occupational specialty so that I could secure employment in the field of electronics and technology. As a woman, I knew this would increase my job and salary opportunities. This proved successful when I landed the job at Lockheed Martin on my return home from Saudi.

But this time, I felt an urge to go back to school. I had no idea what I would take. I had actually moved to Atlanta a few months before my partner's arrival to begin school at a local technical college. I enrolled in an electrical engineering program. The experience seemed awkward. I struggled in the computer-aided drafting class. To draw something in 3D, a person would need to have an acute ability to visualize a three-perspective object. While I like the fact that I was learning computer drafting, I spent an inordinate amount of time in the mechanical drawing lab. Thankfully, the universe sent me some help in both the drawing class and the C++ programing class. God always sends us help, and this has been my experience my entire life—even while I was in the desert.

Sometimes we have to try things on to see how they feel and then see where it takes us. I took this initial path of electrical engineering because my methodical mind was leading me. It was a decision based on my logical brain. I had thought maybe I would enjoy designing electrical circuits The more we are in alignment with God and the universe, the more we have access to our higher spiritual nature. It is in this plane that we are able to connect with our spiritual minds and our higher souls. The apostle Paul calls this mind our "Christ" mind. It would be easy to not make any move at all rather than live in fear that we would make the "wrong" choice. However, this kind of thinking is of the old fear-based paradigm. There is no wrong decision—only experiences in our lives. Just because something is difficult doesn't mean it isn't our path. When I look back on all the jobs, education, and experiences along my life's path, I realize that all of these experiences were teaching me something that I would eventually need to fulfill my soul's purpose work.

Nevertheless, while attending the technical college, I knew that I was not in alignment with my higher purpose. Although I don't think I would have phrased it like this back then, I knew something didn't feel right. I remember the energy that I felt during my time in school seemed awkward. Even though I couldn't articulate it back then as an energy incongruence, I could tell that I was not in alignment with my soul's path. When we are in alignment to our higher selves, we feel more joy, love, contentment, and connection to the energies around us. Later, I learned that I am a healer. Healers are able to feel subtle differences in energy. This gift is immensely helpful as we negotiate life's choices along our path. When we begin to feel stagnant, unhappy, and not fulfilled, we should perform a systems check similar to the helicopter's system power-on check. Which systems on board our bodies are feeling out of alignment? Are we not feeling grounded or secure? Are we operating out of fear-based reasons, such as staying at a job in fear that we will not get another job or opportunity as good as our current job? Stagnant energy can influence our abundance in our current life. It is a good practice to keep the flow of energy clean and moving. We should also become mindful of our living and workspace energy flow. We should prepare these spaces to be in free alignment and not cluttered. The practice of feng shui is vital to keeping energy in our lives liberated. Energy is a consciousness and has awareness.

Technology of Education

Remember the universe has your back. It supports you and affirms you as you move along your planned path to higher unfoldment. To make my point, the minute I decided to leave my engineering education was my turning point to something greater. The universe did not reward me with answers, direction, or even signs until I had the courage to try something different. As soon as I made the move to return to teaching, something shifted and like magic my life was synchronized. My very first day of substituting was when I was introduced to the technology teacher. He invited me to his classroom and after observing all the technical gadgets, I was intrigued. At the time, technology education was a new program in Georgia's school system. There happened to be a technology exposition that weekend, and he invited me to attend. I followed the excitement in my heart, and when I arrived at the event, it lit my soul on fire. I couldn't help but to follow this path because the flame was ever bright in my soul.

After attending the technology exhibition, I felt as if I was on some sort of natural high. When I returned to my partner parents' house, all of a sudden I became chatty Cathy. I could not keep silent about the experience. Even my partner's mom commented on how talkative I had become. This feeling was surely a sign pointing the way to my next experience in life.

While at the technology expo, I met a wonderful and encouraging professor. We spoke about the program and the requirements for admission at Georgia Southern University. He indicated that I would need to take the Graduate Record Exam. This concerned me because

I was not what you would call the academic type. But it was required so I scheduled the exam. Like most of us when we are faced with hurdles, we stress, but there isn't any reason to worry because what is meant to happen will happen. I took the GRE, and the results were a bit low. However, the professor, who was very personal, encouraged me and told me not to worry. He interceded in my behalf with the admissions office and encouraged them to approve my application on a temporary or provisional basis.

Our souls really do know the way, and to figure out our path, we must be willing to follow its inspiration. I was desperately searching for a path that resonated with my soul, and I found it. Shortly after being approved for the program, my partner and I found a quaint, little house that overlooked a lake. It was exciting to finally have a space of our own as we began our new lives in Atlanta. She interviewed and obtained a job in the insurance field, and we manage to find an open and affirming Methodist church that embraced our loving gay lifestyle. For the first time in an open setting, we felt embraced and loved for who we were. The pastor at this particular church had a vision one day as the Pride Parade marched past his church, and he felt God saying to him, "These are your people." The church was dying with an older congregation who could no longer care for the building maintenance or financial obligation. For the first time in my life, I felt safe enough to live authentically, at least while we were visiting the church. This particular church became our family.

We attended church on Sunday morning and Bible study on Thursday nights. It was a freeing experience to be embraced as a couple and addressed that way in conversation. One of the clues that a church or other institution is open and affirming is the way conversation is structured in bulletins, announcements, and face-to-face gatherings. An establishment can say that they embrace diversity, but until an outward blending of affirming is demonstrated, it is mere talk and insincere. A true acceptance of inclusion is exhibited outwardly through all aspects of life—in our verbal conversations, brochures, announcements, etc. These actions demonstrate hearts that love and appreciate God's various creations, even if those creations are different from our own understanding. We are not to judge our brothers and sisters. Nor are we to force them to act in normative binary ways. This constricts the person they came in to express or become.

Nevertheless, this was a new experience for me. I felt loved and included and not treated as if I were an abomination to God. Diversity and inclusion is a relatively new concept within the last twenty years. Thank God for people who feel called to liberate those on the margins of society. Isn't that what the Master Jesus taught? More and more institutions, businesses, and schools are embracing those who identify on the margins. The fight for an egalitarian society has taken millions of years, and we still haven't arrived. My father attended my seminary graduation and made an astute observation. It dawned on him that I was "out" in seminary. I am not sure what transpired to inform him of this, but it was probably in conversations around campus as he interacted with people. Later, he came to me and said something like this: "Hey, all these people know you are a lesbian?" To which I said, "Yes, Dad. They all know." Isn't it wonderful to be included in a group of people and not have to hide who I am? This statement of living authentically was also my requirement when I answered God's call as a pastor. I felt strongly about serving God, but I also wanted to be honest and open about who I was as a lesbian.

As my partner and I settled into our new home, I began working on my master's degree in technology education. My initial studies began at Georgia Southern University. My very first class was a computer numeric controls (CNC) production class. Ironically, CNC is a type of milling program that was very similar to that of my computer-aided drafting program in my electrical engineering program. But this time, the programing language consisted only of three axes (x, y, and z). The machine moves left, right, forward, backward, up, and down to control the depth motion. Remember when I said, "Just because something is difficult doesn't mean it isn't your path"? Well, this machining class really challenged me! I have to laugh now, but it is a good thing I was introduced to these concepts before arriving to my new CNC programming class. I spent all day on these projects. I can't remember the exact requirements of my very first machining project, but I do remember that the spindle had to incorporate a simple linear cut, a circular cut, and a countersunk hole. The design had to include various spindle movements.

The first design had to be handwritten. For the entire three months or so, all I did was work on this machining class. Thankfully, once again, God sent help! The professor was very helpful and allowed me to come in as many times as I needed to complete projects. The next project was more difficult. The end product was machined out of aluminum, I do believe. This class wasn't something that was easy for me. I had to work at it and learn new and different concepts. I would need to understand these concepts as a technology teacher. At the end of the course, I received an A, and I had never been so proud. There is a difference between studying for an academic test and having to perform a project for a grade. While attending Georgia Southern, I learned that I could transfer to the University of Georgia to complete my degree in technology education. Things work out the way they are intended. This is just one example. To be honest, I didn't realize that the University of Georgia offered the program, but I was glad they did because it was closer and I could complete the program sooner.

University of Georgia

Once my Georgia Southern grades were posted, I applied to the University of Georgia as a transfer student. The good news here is that I had earned an A+ in my CNC production class from GSU, and I am certain this achievement helped me to secure enrollment to the University of Georgia. I couldn't believe it! A girl from a small town who graduated high school with an average grade point average and was nearly sent home with a 1.9 GPA from the small college that I had attended in south Florida was now attending UGA. This was a huge accomplishment for me. I had never considered college as a possibility, and now, here I was in a college that ranked in the top three in the nation for its technology education program. I couldn't believe that I was accepted to an elite school. When we follow the prompting of our gut or intuition, the spirit has much more freedom in guiding us to our soul's higher aspirations. This intuition sits deep within our hearts. We really are so much greater when we look to understand our real divine identity. Our divine identity is a higher version of ourselves and very different from our exterior personality. I never even considered going to college. I didn't even know it was possible. When we get out of our own way, we can achieve so much more.

I didn't achieve these things on my own. There are people in our lives who have agreed to help us along the way. For example, our lovers, family, and friends come in with us and agree to either help us achieve what we came here to do, teach us soul lessons, or both. My then partner certainly had a major influence in my academic success. Her writing abilities were better than mine. She possessed the ability and skill to articulate and express a thought or idea more fluently. She was also talented in constructing appropriate sentences while applying correct grammar. She spent nights of her own time helping me draft papers. I remember she and I would be up until midnight completing papers. I would explain the subject matter, and she would improve the structure, readability, and flow of the paper. She was a crucial influence in helping me overcome my lack of confidence in the academic arena. The more time we spent correcting these papers, the more I learned how to write. Her loving support not only taught me how to become a better writer, but her love also helped me to believe in myself. The countless hours she spent helping me with my MEd was a momentous sacrifice that prepared me for my next academic experience. At some level, I believe we planned to share in teaching each other lessons along our path. This thought is one that I ascribed after my spiritual awakening. It is important to understand that the soul chooses its lessons. The soul knows what it needs to work on, and it would be advantageous for the soul's evolution to learn what it has preplanned so that it can accomplish the lessons in this lifetime. Listen to your soul! It knows the way!

Integrating Life

Life really got busy with the two of us working full time, spending nights on papers and scheduling time with my partner's mom. As our parents age, additional care is needed in accomplishing daily routines. As a care provider, it can become difficult to balance our regular daily lives while at the same time caring for our loved ones. These challenges provide opportunities for our souls to grow and learn. Playing the role as a caretaker has a great propensity in teaching us how to practice compassion, love, and mercy. We are challenged greatly to continue offering our kindness and patience even in the midst of our already hectic life demands. Showing someone love, mercy, and compassion usually requires an action. We must offer an extension of ourselves a hug, a conversation, or something else that we act out. This may include making a trip to the grocery store or pharmacy to pick up essential items. These situations are challenging, especially as medical situations present themselves as urgent.

At the core of our makeup, for the most part, we want to help people. But when this help lasts for an expanded length of time, it can become challenging especially when long-term care is required. Keep in mind that these experiences are teaching us something, and it would be advisable for the personality to find out what the soul is seeking to learn in order to reach the next level. If interested, I would suggest seeking a spiritual medium who deals with "prebirth planning" and maybe even "between life soul regression." The soul regressions are most helpful when we seek the lesson's attempted in the past life. Our past lives usually influence our current life experiences especially if we are seeking to accomplish a particular lesson. The important thing to remember here is learning the lesson and not getting so caught up in the past life. Lingering there is not helpful per se, but it can point us in the right direction in helping us to uncover our souls' learning contract for this life.

My partner and I tried to integrate our lives in the community as much as possible. We both joined a local tennis team and played tennis on Saturdays. This was a wonderful and loving experience. The people we met became our family and support. We not only played tennis together, but the team would also schedule short trips to Saint Simon to share some quality time together. We would play games, play tennis, shop, and eat crab bisque. This was my first experience of living authentically with a mixed group of people. Everyone on the team knew that we were partners. They embraced us as a couple. It was a phenomenal experience to be loved and accepted by others even though we were gay. My partner had lived a much freer and open life than I did. She knew early on who she was and came out of the proverbial closet as a teenager. On the other hand, it took me longer to figure out who I was sexually. Initially, I tried to fit into the heterosexual lifestyle, but I never really connected with this type of relationship. It would take me falling in love with my partner to have the courage to venture outside the current acceptable social norms.

Although I was very comfortable sharing my sexual orientation and same-sex relationship with our tennis team, it was quite another to feel safe enough to share this information with people in my school system. It was a chance that I wasn't willing to take. After all, I would be putting my personal life out there for people of a lower vibration to judge. Humanity's spiritual evolution is in the tail end of the fifth "Root Race," meaning that most of my coworkers at the time were not awakened enough to understand fluid-binary concepts. For the most part, my colleagues only understood sexual orientation and gender roles as a duality. This means that they ascribed to a belief that life has to be lived a particular way to be accepted. Looking at life this way constricts our Creator. God made both day and night but also created dawn and dusk. We have a tendency to put limits on God. Understanding life only in the terms of duality causes people to judge anything that falls outside those norms as morally wrong or bad.

Root Races are evolutionary cycles whereby humanity evolves along a continuum progression. There are seven Root Races, and thankfully we are slowly evolving into the sixth. Each Root Race is then divided into seven subraces. This is an esoteric belief and worth the exploration. If studied, it will explain the unfoldment of humankind's origin and evolutionary path. For the most part, humanity grows collectively, although we are blessed to encounter higher evolved souls who incarnate for the purpose of helping humanity evolve to the next higher spiritual level. It takes a long time to advance the evolutionary path of humankind. I would continue living a closeted life in the school system while for the most part my partner chose to live her life courageously open in her various job roles. From the onset of our relationship, she always chose to live authentically. For the most part, people that she encountered seemed to be both open and accepting of our relationship. Her two brothers were always accepting and treated us as partners. My partner's loving nature couldn't believe that there might be people out there looking for opportunities to demonstrate malice because of their lack of understanding.

As life continued to unfold for us in Atlanta, we did the best we could to balance our relationship with scheduled trips and fun outings while also trying to maintain our obvious responsibilities. We spent Thanksgiving and Christmas holidays at my family's home in Florida. For the most part, my family responded to our relationship in a more covert way. Our relationship wasn't really discussed in my family. My father was more overt about his disapproval. His stance, I am sure, was influenced by our Catholic religious roots. Although my family knew about our relationship, they never asked direct questions about our life together as partners! The gay lifestyle wasn't something new to my family as I have a younger sister who came out during her teens.

Although the gay lifestyle for the most part was new to most families in the sixties, queer relationships have been around for millenniums. If we study the evolution of human sexuality, we will find that humanities earlier forms were androgynous. See Aristotle's "One Sex Theory" if interested. Unfortunately, society creates acceptable and unacceptable social norms based on their lack of understanding human sexuality and evolution.

The problem with developing ethical behaviors based on current social norms is that this approach assumes that human sexuality is fixed and binary. This construct believes that humans do not change or evolve, especially their sexuality. One thing I believe we can all agree on is that everything is changing and evolving. When we refuse to change, we die. When social norms are used as a consideration to develop ethical behaviors, it creates a fear-based society. When we see difference as fear, it begins to compartmentalize who's accepted and who is not. This creates walls that divide us. Fear drives shame in our society when we don't measure up to social standards. We need to teach that it is OK to embrace sexuality and sexual expression differently even if that expression is considered counterculture. As long as we are expressing God in a loving way and treating others with love, we should all have the latitude to express our identity freely. We each have a unique expression of our Creator, and that is why we come here as Cocreators.

It should be understood that my generation wasn't the first generation to have gay people. By no means. Same-sex relationships have been around since the beginning of time. Culture norms and religious dogma determine what is acceptable and unacceptable behavior in social settings. Humanity is just now evolving to a higher mental and spiritual awareness of human sexuality. This understanding has allowed those who identify as LGBTQ+ to express themselves openly. The Stonewall Uprising in Greenwich Village, New York, during 1969 had a major influence in helping the gay community gain their freedom in public spaces. This was a profound movement that was a huge contributing factor in liberating and transforming acceptable social norms for the lesbian, gay, bi, transgender, and queer (LGBTQ+) community. How could I expect my family to understand me as a lesbian? At the time, I didn't even understand it.

I would find later that my queer identity is the very thing that sent me in search of a loving and accepting God. God uses what we consider defects to make us push through self-limiting beliefs, and once we get beyond these, we realize that we are so much more than the labels that society gives us. It really does get down to limiting beliefs. Humanity sets limiting beliefs, not God. These lower beliefs occur because people and social communities lack spirituality, which leads to achieving a higher consciousness or higher truth. To make my point, Native Americans gave honor to individuals who identified as LGBT+. The Native Americans referred to them as "two spirited" people. These people were seen as "gifted." They were often the tribes' shamans and spiritual leaders.

CHAPTER FOUR

⁓⁓

A Stressful Homecoming

In 2001, my partner and I would finally make a bold decision to move to Florida. We had discussed the possibility of moving to Florida at various times over the years, and we finally felt that it was the right time. So we began the process of listing our house. Through networking, we were introduced to a small real estate agency so we listed with them. We signed the necessary paperwork and began the waiting game. Thankfully, we only signed a three-month contract and those three months came and went and we still had no offers.

It didn't seem that anyone was interested in purchasing real estate during that time. We didn't even have one house showing. Every month that our house was listed put additional stress on our already dismal finances, and it was beginning to take a toll on our relationship as well. Another factor to consider for the house not selling quickly was that the lending institutions were cracking down on loan qualifications. If memory serves me right, there had been a lot of loans extended to people who were not really qualified to fulfill loan agreements. This caused the financial industry to implement stricter requirements for home buying, making it more difficult to get a loan for those outside the "A" credit identifier.

We both liquidated all assets, to include our whole-life insurance policies and other bank accounts. We pulled from any and all accounts to keep the mortgage payment current. Over the months, our reserves became depleted and we were forced to lean on help from family members to get us through this difficult time. Having to rely on other people in any situation brings an opportunity for humility. That is for sure. These situations help us to be compassionate to others who find themselves in hard times. When we have similar experiences as others, we are more compassionate about their situations. If we take a look at all the organizations created in the world, we can see that a lot of these are created as a result of people experiencing suffering. There are several support groups to help those struggling with addiction issues or for single mothers struggling to raise their children, and the list goes on. There is an opportunity for all of us to give back to a need or a cause. To find that cause, we can take a look at where our passions intersect a need in the community and begin there.

Experiences like mine help us to understand that sometimes unemployment can happen to anyone. Society likes to put labels on the unemployed. Society has a habit of labeling people out of work as lazy or people who are not willing to work for a living. I can say that my experience has helped me to be more compassionate for those who are struggling to make ends meet. As for my situation, I could only ignore the mortgage company's phone calls for a limited time. At one point, we were three months in arrears. The mortgage company really wasn't much help either. One time, the mortgage company agreed to let us make two split payments in one month but sum payment of the two had to suffice the monthly mortgage payment. To me, this didn't make any sense at all. If we didn't have the money to make a one-time monthly payment, we certainly didn't have the money to make two payments in one month.

This time in our lives really became stressful. I have never experienced such a tough time getting employment. There were no jobs. My partner took a sales position in the beginning that was commission only, and bless her heart, she tried to make it work. I don't know how people with these kinds of sales jobs survive. We were counting on our house in Atlanta to sell quickly, but that did not happen. It got so tight that we didn't have the money to pay for rent so we had to move. Remember nothing happens by accident. Thankfully, one of her sales appointments was with an older lesbian couple, and they invited us to live in their home. Thank God, because I don't know what we would have done. We might have been on the streets.

Once we moved in, we were able to switch our attention full time to job hunting. In a way, this shifted our energy. Sometimes all we need is a shift in energy to turn things around. This shift allowed us to stop focusing on our lack and directed us to begin cocreating with God to begin manifesting something new. New jobs. Our new friends showered us with love and provided us with a roof over our heads and cooked meals. We tried to offer them gratitude for their hospitality and offered to work in the yard and house as needed. While we were there, we cleaned and fix things that might have been broken. One time our friends' washing machine broke, and we were able to fix it, and another time, we built a porch. We gave back when possible.

It was during this time that we also relisted our house with a larger real estate company, and we truly focused on just getting through each day. The stress was causing friction in our relationship. I wish that I had been more spiritually aware during those days to realize that everything happens for a reason and in every exercise is a lesson. Perhaps the very lesson that our soul picked before arriving here. I also wished that I had known about the universal laws back then. I didn't realize that the more I stressed, the more stress would enter my life. The more that I focused on lack, the more the universe delivered me lack. I was like a spider weaving my own web of misfortunes.

I focused too much on the possible default of our loan when I should have focused more on finding positive ways of strengthening our relationship. I also should have learned how to meditate and practice mindfulness. These practices have been proven to increase our vibration, moods, and situation. Meditation teaches us self-awareness and how to stay in the present moment. Like I said, I focused too much on the physical situation instead of turning inward to seek spiritual guidance.

My partner and I continued to network at church and other social gatherings to help put the word out that we were in need of jobs. A year and a few months had passed since I returned home, and finally, I was offered an interview and secured a job in November 2002. Life really is about energy movement. A few more months would pass, and in April 2003, our house in Atlanta would finally sell. I never would have imagined that it would take a year and a half to sell our home and get jobs. But it did!

I made a trip to Atlanta to take care of the necessary closing paperwork and last-minute repairs. God sends people to help us just at the right time. Our closing Realtor was a godsend. I can't remember the fine details, but I do recall that I was short on some of the closing cost, and she covered it. The details are foggy here, but I believe after closing I returned her money, and if I remember correctly, she told me to keep it.

Shortly after the house sold, my partner got another sales position with what seemed to be a reputable communications company. We were happy that her new sales position wasn't a commission-only offer. However, once she was there a few months, unrealistic sales demands were soon placed on her. The company began setting unreasonable sales goals that caused some of her coworkers to become creative in their sells pitches. She would spend more time undoing deceitful sells to the elderly who had no use for a more technical sells package. My partner was doing the right thing by following her heart to align those customers with phone service that was more in line with their usage.

Her heart was in the right place, but this caused grief with her superiors because she fell behind in her sales performance. This job ended up being very stressful. Our jobs play a big part in our lives. They can cause us to live very unhappy lives. Unfortunately, most businesses are only concerned about their revenues. This is the old Piscean age concept, and now that the age of Aquarius has arrived, we should be seeing more of the heart and spiritual presenting itself in the world. I might add here that because of our recent hostile events in Ukraine that the transition from the old Piscean age to the new age (new earth) isn't going to happen overnight. It will take every light worker out there to shine their love light. Any transition will take more of humankind to awaken to their higher selves before a global awakening can occur. Meanwhile, the world continues to suffer at the hands of those who are not awakened to their true selves.

Our entire lives revolve around relationships. Our jobs consume most of our waking hours, and they can become stressful if we do not understand the laws of the universe. Our jobs provide us with unique relationship experiences outside our partners and family. We intermingle with various types of people at work. Our jobs provide us with interpersonal experiences. At work, we interact with all different types of people. These interactions can become challenging as well. We spend half of our lives at work. During this time, we are faced with many opportunities for growth. Sometimes we cling to jobs that are no longer serving us. We become unhappy at work but fear leaving the financial security. Remaining at jobs that are dysfunctional and at times hostile influences our daily peace and harmony with the universe. When we are out of alignment with the universe, we become imbalanced, and this imbalance can affect all kinds of things, such as our health, our relationships, and our financial abundance. Negotiating these situations requires spiritual awareness and soul intuition. These are not easy situations to negotiate.

My partner and I were at our lowest. We had a lot to try to negotiate. The job situation and lack of money was taking a toll on our relationship. On top of the stress already mentioned, my partner was trying her best to care for her mom. She loved her mom and tried to support her mom in the most loving ways. Time is the most precious gift we can offer others. My partner spent a lot of time with her mom. Although their relationship at times was difficult, my partner remained close and loving to her mother. She would spend time watching television, cooking, shopping, and helping to clean her mom's house. And at other times, she would take her to her various appointments, such as her hair appointment and of course to her doctor. These actions show tremendous love even during tumultuous times. My partner loved her mom and others selflessly. Sometimes these situations can be difficult to negotiate because we have to also learn how to care for ourselves while caring for others. I have nothing but the utmost respect for my partner's love and commitment to her mother.

Some believe that we pick our mothers before we come to this place called earth. Mothers offer us lessons while in the physical. Many of these lessons occur before we reach adulthood. It might be difficult to accept this idea, but these relationships are the most profound in our lives even through our adult years. A mother's relationship with her child is one of the most influential relationships that we will ever have in our lives, except with our partners. It is important to learn what we can and let the rest go. Forgiving and releasing past traumas can be the greatest gift that we give ourselves. The soul becomes trapped when we remain unforgiving and bitter the rest of our lives. For the soul's sake, we should try to implement this concept of forgiving and releasing. It is critical to liberate the soul from its lower nature. The unwillingness to love, forgive, and move on will create karma in our own lives. There is liberation on the other side of our trauma, but most of us choose to wallow in our unfortunate woes. Believing we are victims and powerless sends a signal to the universe that we believe these lower truths and therefore the universe will continue sending what we are putting out. The unwillingness to forgive and release is the worst thing that we can do as it causes the soul to sit in a lower vibration without a way forward to liberate itself to a higher vibration. We really do waste our precious lives when we sit around and focus on our misfortunes. I say this through experience.

CHAPTER FIVE

Relationship Crumbles

My relationship with my partner finally ended shortly after Christmas of 2005. I remember this because Hurricane Ivan had hit a few months before her leaving. We had pulled apart, and it was difficult to regain the relationship. I have to own part of this breakup. I certainly could have done a better job. The soul comes here with a plan in mind with our lovers. Why do we act in nonloving ways when we are here in the physical? It is because we are not awakened and the soul is still growing. The soul seeks to find itself in the spiritual spark; however, until it wakes up to its higher spiritual self, the ego runs the show in this 3D space we call earth. This is why is so important to "wake up" while we are here in the physical. When the ego leads, it does things to hurt other people.

Most of us have no clue that our egos are running the show while we are in the physical. Have you ever done something and then later asked yourself, "Why did I do that?" Well, I have too. The answer to this question is that the soul is not awakened and living into its higher self. Without a spiritual awakening, we are operating from our lower selves. Said another way, we are living in bondage to our egos. I want to add another point here. It is easy to place blame in situations here on earth. This attitude is not helpful to the soul's ascension. The soul really does know the way! When the personality gets stuck, it jeopardizes the soul's opportunity for advancement. The soul will strongly urge the personality to continue moving forward in an upward and positive fashion; however, without the awareness of the soul's prompting, we are oblivious to the soul's divine guidance.

Grief, Hurt, and Pain

My breakup was the most devastating event that I have ever had to endure. It was more traumatic than my experience in Desert Storm. Life for me during that time was excruciating. The experience was unbearable at times. My heart was in so much pain that I thought I would never recover. During the first year, I lived on Oreo cookies and beer. I don't know how I made it through work. I took a lot of time off. I was an emotional wreck both during and after work hours. For me, life had ended. My heart was traumatized, and it was hurting. I could not visualize a meaningful life without the love of my life. When we experience these kinds of deep sufferings, they have a way of breaking us or causing us to experience an awakening or spiritual rebirth.

For me, this awakening would take several years to unfold after the initial traumatic loss. During those five years, I was forced to look inward and gain strength from a part of me that I didn't know existed. In the beginning, I lived a secluded life. I didn't venture out except to go to work. I stopped attending church. Breakups are hard on friends as they feel that they should choose a side. We are programmed to assign blame to the ending of a relationship; however, I think a better, more productive approach is to figure out where the learning is in the experience and learn the lesson so that it doesn't repeat itself. If we knew what lessons we came here to learn, I think it would be better to seek out the learning instead of the loss. I mourned the loss of this relationship for five years. This experience caused my soul to pause until I was finally able to find the spirit within me, which was my compass to my higher spiritual self.

CHAPTER SIX

Seeking a Way Forward

This time in my life was painful and downright unbearable. I lacked direction, especially forward direction. My heart always wanted to go backward as it could see no benefit from moving forward. For most of those five years, I was in quicksand and my lower nature refused any possible future without my partner. However, as the years unfolded, I had to make a decision to remain broken and depressed or choose to begin living and creating a new life.

Several years after my breakup, I purposely sought people who might need some support in their own lives. This would force me out of myself and into other people's lives. I kept myself busy helping others and providing support in any way that I could. I would offer to use my talents of fixing and remodeling to help these folks that were also hurting. When we begin to focus on others, somehow our own hurts are not primary. In the midst of helping others, I gained friendship and a good feeling for helping them during their own crises. God or the Universe always sends people to help us out during our lowest moments. I didn't have a lot of friends, but I did gain some vital lifelong friendships along the way.

When we are not awakened to why bad things happen to us, It is easy to withdraw and focus on the poor-me syndrome. When we do this, what we are really saying to the universe is that we are powerless. During the soul's life on earth, the soul plans certain experiences to help it grow. This includes relationship issues or challenges as a result of living this life together in partnerships. I would like to stress here to refrain from placing blame on anything that we may experience in this life. It is easy to point fingers and to point blame for our circumstances, but in doing so, we miss our learning objective. I wasted a lot of time in my depression. My soul finally guided me. More likely, I finally began listening to my inward compass, my soul; it began guiding me to seek new and different spiritual experiences. I knew religious dogma, but I didn't understand anything spiritual.

The soul prompted me to venture out of my comfort zone by attending spiritual classes and events. I joined a local spiritual group and met other people who were also seeking to *know thyself.* This knowing is always understood spiritually. I attended spiritually enriching social events, workshops, and small gatherings. While I felt very uncomfortable attending, I had to constantly push the ego to attend these spiritual gatherings. The ego didn't want to attend, and it tried to give all kinds of excuses. One of these excuses was the class was too expensive and I could use that money to pay bills. Another excuse was that this spiritual stuff was way out in left field and I'd better get back to my religious roots. The excuses kept coming, but my higher self continued to push the envelope around spiritual development. The spiritual leader was quite knowledgeable and very interested in helping people to grow into their higher selves. There was a passion to help people awaken to their higher selves. The path to achieving higher awareness requires the mind to slow down so that it can hear that still, small voice deep within whispering higher knowledge. I can't really speak for the spiritual mentor, but looking back now, it seems this is the purpose.

It is the strangest thing that the ego never wants to grow and is always content living on the lower plane. Until we experience an awakening, we seriously have no idea that our egos are controlling us. These spiritual classes were helping me heal and advancing my consciousness. I was able to meet new and unique friends. Many of these individuals were on their own spiritual journey. There was something different about them. They seemed more sincere and heart centered than the average person. Although these spiritual classes were very uncomfortable in the beginning, something inside me encouraged me to continue showing up at the class. These classes began to open a side of me that I never knew existed. We were introduced to all kinds of things such as our energetic systems in our bodies. These energetic systems are also called chakras, and they control the energetic flow in our bodies. We were introduced to each energetic center and learned their particular importance. We were also taught how to align and balance them.

One time, we met and paired off in twos and practiced developing our intuition. We were also introduced to the concept of energy healing. One popular form of healing is Reiki, but there are several techniques to inquire. Other forms of healing, such as working with aromatherapy, acupuncture, stones, meditation, and other ancient wisdom techniques, were presented in class. While we didn't perform these techniques, we were introduced to their effectiveness for healing ourselves and those individuals we were called to help. It was during this class that I was told that I was a gifted healer; however, I initially blew it off because I wasn't familiar with the efficaciousness of the various healing modalities at the time, and I was swamped with seminary assignments that prevented me from pursuing the spiritual path earlier in life. I wished that I had awakened earlier in my life; there is a lot of the ancient wisdom still yet to learn. They are life altering and offer us a path to better spiritual, physical, and mental health.

In these spiritual gatherings, we learned a lot of new and interesting spiritual concepts that I had never considered. Although I was interested in learning how to heal, I wasn't sure which practice was the best. I labored for a few years researching the various healing techniques. I figured if I was going to heal people, I wanted to learn the closest method to the divine. In my research, I had come across a type of healing called *sekhem*. This energy modality is said to be connected with ancient Egypt and the star system Sirius. I would like to stress here for the reader that these classes were not necessarily about the personality's desire for education or academics. It was much deeper than this. It was my soul guiding and leading me to my higher self. The spiritual classes and gatherings were my soul's way of introducing me to the ancient mysteries that I have always known but have forgotten. We are so much more than our personalities. It is wild how the soul guides the personality, but to accomplish this, we must overcome our lower nature so that we can begin experiencing these higher vibrations. It is in these higher vibrations where we are able to discern our higher nature. The spiritual path requires courage, but we cannot have courage without a direction and purpose. It is our purpose that keeps us moving forward and faith believing that we will accomplish that still, small voice deep within us.

We all have a purpose in life. We come into this world with an inkling of a passion that we planned on the other side before we got here. Unfortunately, when we arrive here, we become immersed into the physical: paying bills, raising children, taking care of others, etc. Without awakening to a higher knowing, we forget the reason for our arrival to this earth school. It is easy for the unconscious mind to fall prey to self-limiting beliefs that keep us in bondage to our material world and old beliefs. I also want to stress the importance of divine willpower while we are here trying to accomplish the soul's goals. Nothing in life is easy, especially when we find ourselves always swimming upstream in a world that is still practicing harmful social binary construct from the last Piscean age. In many ways, we are taught that if something doesn't come easy to us then maybe it isn't our intended path. I never could understand why humanity had to be so unkind. Many times I found myself in hostile, controlling environments and wondered why life had to be so difficult. It was much later into my adulthood that I began to understand that each soul is at a level of maturity, and this reflects in their behaviors. It doesn't mean that a particular path isn't ours to take. It may be a difficult path we choose to help bring in the light for a particular group of souls.

The Piscean age encouraged a warrior-type society where the unhealthy masculine energy was valued over the healthy feminine qualities. Women were seen only as child bearers. Men were highly valued, and it was acceptable for a person, especially a man, to become a toxic leader who asserted control over others by displaying negative emotions of anger and violence. Men were placed in charge of families, and women had no rights. I remember this to be true because my mom tells me a story that after my parents had the four of us, she wanted a hysterectomy but had to seek my father's permission first. If I remember correctly, my father had to sign a medical release form from my mother's doctor as a way of authorizing her surgery. I find this appalling and an impingement on an individual's "free will" to choose their own path or way forward. This is a prime example of how women and other marginalized groups are held into oppression by the majority's constructs of lower truths. Currently in society, major heteronormative groups determine what are acceptable and not acceptable behaviors.

These are the kinds of beliefs that hold the soul captive to its lower nature. This is why it takes courage, purpose, faith, and divine wisdom to show us the way to our higher nature. For millennials, we have ignored the feminine energy, and as a result, we have created a highly competitive and toxic, masculine-controlled planet. Jesus and other Spiritual Masters have come here to teach humankind to love more and to learn how to go inward to our center sanctuary. Here we learn patience, love, and how to feel Spirit. Jesus, said, "The kingdom of God is within you." We need healthy feminine energies and higher aspirations to help us discern higher truths. These higher truths are gained through intuition. Emotions can be both toxic and positive. Higher aspirations come from our intuition. Our intuitive feelings, which come from our deepest knowing, are communicative and help us to navigate closer to our called purpose. They help us discern our path and help us to distinguish our lower nature from our higher spiritual nature. The feminine energy does have its lower nature. These harmful feminine energies manifest as manipulation, codependency, insecurity, feeling powerless, and passivity, to name a few. These lower feminine energies are controlled by our egos. We tend to believe we are powerless when in fact we are not.

In order to shift away from the old paradigm and into a higher vibrational earth, we must learn how to balance our energies in a positive sense. The universe is at a tipping point right now. We need more love and compassion to help Mother Gaia move toward her higher vibrations of truth and love. The world must learn how to develop and value the higher feminine energy. This energy is guided by love and compassion, but to get there, we must practice leaning into our intuitive gifts when solving problems. I remember my own oppressive experience growing up in a Catholic family. Boys were always valued more than girls, and girls were considered weak and a liability. Girls were considered "weak" because they tended to lean more on their lower vibrational energies of negative emotions. In many cultures, women were only valued for having male babies.

My intent here is not to badger one energy type against another but to highlight their lower and higher natures so that the reader can learn to recognize lower natures when they appear in relationships around them. The universe will send synchronicities to help us correct our lower energies. Being able to recognize our unbalanced energies allows us an opportunity to correct and then begin healing our energetic system. The masculine and feminine energy is also called the yen and yang energies respectively. These terms originated from the Chinese. It is important to become aware and mindful of what vibrational energies we are manifesting in our persona for reasons already discussed. For those of us truly interested in liberating our souls from this 3D limiting space called earth, attuning and balancing our energy is utmost. Spend the time to recognize and identify blockages, such as limiting beliefs, ideas, and blocked energies. Removing and healing energy deficiencies liberates the soul so that it can return to a higher plane. This place called earth is only a school room. Once we master it, we can return to the divine and ascend to higher dimensions. We come to earth school over and over again to learn how to balance our energies. In one life, we may come in as a female, and in another, we come in as a male. One time we may experience being a mother with children, and another time we may experience being a male with no children. These life lessons are selected by our higher self and our spiritual guides for the purpose of ascending.

We make a plan before arriving to earth, but it doesn't mean that things will unfold exactly as we planned it. In every situation, the personality has a choice, and these choices all lead to new lessons. There isn't really a wrong way, just a different way with different lessons. It is possible that we accomplish our souls' lessons through various paths and experiences than the ones planned. For me, I tried to follow my intuition with each experience that I held in the present moment. Inwardly, if something didn't feel right, I changed my circumstances. Soren Kierkegaard said that life is lived forward but understood backward. Now that I have lived for a while, I can look back and see how my life unfolded and why.

My experiences, like any other person's experiences, began with birth. I had a mom, a dad, and three sisters. As mentioned before,

I believe that I chose my parents in a prebirth planning session before incarnating. I chose my parents for the lessons that I set out to achieve. After graduating from high school, I was playing in a softball tournament and out of nowhere a stranger offered me a softball scholarship. Since there are no accidents, this must have been a prebirth planned event. Hopefully, I will participate in an in-between life regression and find more answers that I am seeking. From my adult view, it seems that every job and experience that I had offered me some form of learning. My softball experience would pave a way for affordable education. I would eventually major in sports science with a focus in K-12 physical education.

Soon after I graduated from college in spring of 1984, I landed a job at the local YMCA and worked as a day camp leader and coordinator. After several years of working this position, I realized that this job was not going to provide me with a secure financial future. I had one opportunity to apply for a physical education position, but I was not hired. I could not understand why I was not hired. I not only was a student at this particular school, but at the time of the interview, I was a student teacher. I just knew that I would land the job and become a physical education coach until retirement. However, this is not how things worked out. I did not get the job. When I asked the principal why, he gave me an unacceptable answer in that the other applicant had more experience and that the beginning teacher paperwork was cumbersome. I was confident that I was an excellent teacher, but I could not compete with work experience. The only experience that I had was my student teaching hours. I was disappointed at the time, but I now know this was *not* my path. This situation led me to sign up for the military. I wanted something more out of life. Something deep within me was nudging me to sign up. My stepfather also encouraged me. The military would provide me with additional training and free education. Military would give me the experience that I was looking for, and it looked good on a resume.

I joined the army and enrolled in the delayed entry program in November 1986, and I left for boot camp in February 1987. I was sent to specialized training in 1988, and then the Desert Storm conflict happened in 1990–91 and I was deployed to Saudi Arabia. As I mentioned earlier, Desert Storm, was a life-altering event. Although it was a traumatizing experience, it would pay off in the future. My military career ended in July 1991 shortly after I returned from Saudi. It was here that I began focusing on additional education through the government Montgomery GI Bill program. I went back to school to obtain certification to teach technology education.

I taught high school technology for about four years. I became disappointed with the system and eventually quit, but I want to point out that this is yet another example of a transition point in life. I enjoyed teaching very much, but my soul was prompting me that it was time to move on. My soul was letting me know that my time there was complete. I spent four good years teaching high school students about the power of believing in themselves and teaching them that they could achieve anything in this world if they oriented their minds to accomplish it. This experience as a teacher also provided me with an opportunity to learn how to teach effectively. It also provided me with practical experience in delivering instruction to a classroom of students. I learned how to create curriculum and lessons that would assist the students in grasping content. I didn't know it at the time, but this experience as a technology education teacher allowed me to practice and develop successful skills for teaching subject content. I also leaned on this experience when I began developing Bible study material and sermon lessons for preaching. Even when we don't understand how things are unfolding, the universe and your soul know the path and the plan. All we have to do is follow. Now I am able to look back and see how each experience prepared me for my called purpose.

Shortly after this transition point, we moved to Pensacola and I obtained a purchasing agent position. I held this position for eight years. It would be the longest position that I ever held consecutively. It seemed that something was pulling me to keep life moving forward. Some people feel called to stay in one job, perhaps as a math teacher until retirement, but I never felt that I should stay in these positions for any length of time so I kept moving forward. I was following some sort of innate compass inside me. My soul! At eight years, my purchasing agent position was becoming turbulent. The job was becoming hostile.

Hostile Working Conditions

At this time, I was beginning to feel uncomfortable at work. Things were beginning to become hostile, and it became a struggle to continue going to work. It seemed that life around me was crumbling. Not only did my relationship collapse, but now my job was disintegrating. What I didn't know was that life was preparing me for a major transition in my life. I continued to hold on to my job, hoping that the hostile environment would pass and hoping that some people would transition to other positions or to new jobs. But when that didn't happen, I was forced to reevaluate my next move. I didn't know what to do, but when I was called aside for a disciplinary write-up, I knew that my time there was nearing an end. I wished that I had known about how energy moves and shifts in polarity. These energetic vibrations are helpful as the fluctuations guide the soul along its planned path. when this happened; Understanding the ebb and flow of energy would have helped me negotiate these kinds of life events more effectively. I could have used these events to guide my soul but instead I acted as if I was being unjustly attacked when in fact it was the universe letting me know it was time to move on.

I finally acquiesced and began to methodically prepare my exit plan. I packed a box and put the company's name on the box, and when the time felt right, I would fill the box with the appropriate items such as uniforms then address the box and look for the appropriate time to quit. As with any decision in life, rash decisions are never good. We need to learn how to commune with God, our higher selves, and our spiritual guides in order to make the best decision possible. I had already been in prayer and in constant communication with spirit about this decision and was confident that I was making the right decision. Seeking truth takes time. I will admit that initially I was caught up in the injustice of my write-up. It bothered me that I was being singled out and targeted for something I didn't deserve. Beware this is the ego seeking justice, so to speak. Truth only seeks to guide us to truth. It doesn't need existential justice. It is justice.

The Call

When we begin to understand things from a higher frequency, we begin to understand that things in our life like jobs and relationships have a beginning and an end. In order to embrace my higher call, I had to leave my current job. It is easier to leave a job that we are unhappy with than a job where we love showing up every day. The hostile environment was a catalyst that helped me move in a higher direction. When the right time presented itself, I prepared the box and filled it with the appropriate items and mailed the box with my resignation letter to the company.

If you are experiencing a turbulent situation, it may be that a change is due in your life. Endings are not bad; they leave room for new beginnings, growth, and space for renewed energy. Turbulent situations force us to focus on life's current issues. These issues may be disguised as encouragement to move forward in life. Endings can be either turbulent or calm nudges that help us focus on our future. Next time that you are experiencing a turbulent situation, remember that it may be the universe guiding you to a higher life calling. A calling that was planned before your arrival here. Transitions should be looked at with a positive outlook, and not something to dread. Everything changes. The law of energy states that energy can neither be created nor destroyed only converted from one form of energy to another (US Energy Information Administration).

I didn't feel this way at the time. I was upset and taking more of a self-defeating attitude. I was wondering why I had to leave my current employer and position. Why me? These thoughts are fear based and hold us back. Soon enough it was obvious that my time was up, I methodically inserted my last uniform shirt into the box, sealed it, and then mailed it to the company. I had spent the last two weeks giving my stuff away to my coworkers who depended on my purchasing expertise. I remember one of them even asking me if I was quitting. In a way, I felt guilty leaving them to rely on someone else to procure their items. But this is chatter in the lower mind that is fearful of trusting God/Universe and moving forward to something greater. We have to know when the time is right to move on in life and believe that there is something greater beyond our misery. We didn't come here to experience misery every time we go to work or home for that matter. After I quit, I actually applied for another purchasing agent position. I even participated in two rounds of interviews, but I finally had the courage to acquiesce to spirit. I had a long conversation with God asking, "What next?" It would be this question that led me to my called purpose work with the church.

CHAPTER SEVEN

Episcopal Divinity School

I prayed and asked for guidance of what my next task may be. I truly didn't know which direction I was going. I followed the inspiration within my soul. This led me first to start a spiritual education counseling program, but that didn't really pan out. The logistics were difficult getting assignments handed in so I began looking for seminary schools. In one of my prayers with God, I had retorted that wherever all this was leading, I wanted to live an authentic life doing it. I scoured the internet for seminary schools that were "open and affirming." I finally found a seminary that embraced authenticity from their applicants, and that was the Episcopal Divinity School (EDS) in Cambridge, Massachusetts. This meant that I could be honest about who I was as a lesbian without risking a rejection letter from the seminary. The school was an independent school that had some latitude in creating progressive and egalitarian liberation curriculum. They also had latitude on approving the applicants for enrollment. It was important to me to be authentic as an out lesbian for the purpose of doing God's work. EDS was a progressive seminary who sought justice and liberation for the marginalized in the community. They taught their preachers to stand against injustice and work to create a just society where all are valued regardless of sexuality, gender, race, creed, or economic status.

EDS seminarians and faculty members were at the forefront fighting liberation for the least of these in our society. They pushed for change and equal rights both inside and outside the church. EDS has a long-standing history in fighting for justice and equality through civil rights marches as well as advocating for LGBTQ+ rights. Three of EDS's faculty members were one among of the Philadelphia Eleven who were the first women ordained in the Episcopal Church..

I applied to the Master of Divinity program at the Episcopal Divinity School in the fall of 2010. EDS was known as a rigorous academic school. They partnered with Harvard, and this allowed EDS students to also take Harvard classes. EDS was also a member of the Boston Theological Institute, where many other seminaries and divinity schools shared resources in the Boston area. When I saw the school's social justice history and the accomplishments of many of their professors, I didn't think I had a chance at being accepted. I was in awe at the highly attuned achievements of both the institution and the faculty members. As I completed the essay portion of my application, I told God it was now in divine hands. Although I had close to a 3.6 GPA while attending the University of Georgia, I was still struggling with confidence as I applied to such an elite school.

A couple of months went by and then I received an email from the EDS admissions team stating that my application had been accepted. It was a surreal experience. I thought, *Only divine intervention could have made this happen.* I was ecstatic. I wasn't sure how I was going to pull this off, but I was going to sure try. I truly didn't have the money or resources to attend such an elite school. There were small grants offered, but for the most part, these classes were funded via loans. The thought of a loan this large in my midlife alarmed me. I thought, *How will I ever pay this loan off?* Taking on such a huge debt wasn't like my me, and then taking on such a huge amount in my late life troubled me. I kept thinking, *How am I going to pay this loan off before I leave this world?* This is one of those examples where the higher self really does know better. It understands the situation and higher possibilities better than the personality does. When we fall prey to our fears, we limit our possibilities and prevent our soul from achieving its higher goals and achieving what it came here to accomplish. Looking at it from this side, I can understand how fear really does immobilize us. It prevents us from achieving higher aspirations of the soul. We make a plan before coming to this plane called earth. And the universe is constantly nudging us to achieve those soul goals that we have set for the purpose of soul growth.

My hostile situation at work was only an avenue to point me to higher blessings and a path toward enlightenment. My acceptance to the Episcopal Divinity School was a path that would eventually lead me to a higher awakening. I am so glad that I listened to that still, small voice inside me. We can call this our intuition, God, or the universe, but in order to hear this voice, we must learn how to separate the chatter or fear from our divine nature. Once we accomplish this, we are able to hear and follow God's divine compass for our lives. It takes intuition, courage, and strength to follow our higher selves, but this is the only path to enlightenment.

I attended the Episcopal Divinity School from 2011 to 2016. It was an amazing experience. I was in awe of the reality that I was actually attending this Ivy League institution. Academically, it would be a challenge for me. In the beginning, it took a couple of weeks to write a six-page paper. My Hebrew Testament professor was requiring one critical essay a week in the beginning. I wasn't accustomed to writing that many papers. Before writing the paper, a lot of exegetical work was required. We read other theologians' work and then synthesized our own understanding of the assigned scripture. With any argument, the writer has to first read countless theologians' work and somehow try to formulate our own understanding about the scripture. The process was arduous. To make matters worse, the resource materials were mostly comparative in nature, meaning that the authors were comparing several theologians' work at once, and I struggled sorting this out in my mind. Organizing my thoughts would present a challenge in my assignments, but I kept going.

In the beginning, I needed every hour of the day to complete my assignments. Many of the other students would meet outside school hours to spend time together. They were building relationships through laughter, relaxation, and of course eating. I remember one time that I had to leave a get-together because I was worried about not completing an assignment. My first three years of seminary, I lived like a hermit. I rarely went out for entertainment or food consumption. Instead, I chose to stay on campus and eat the prepared meal plan that was offered on campus. Many of my colleagues were making time to enjoy a Red Sox game or visit downtown Boston and catch up on the tourist attractions. Boston's subway system was massive and I was challenged navigationally. Therefore, I chose closer places to explore that were within walking distance, such as Cambridge and Harvard. Coming from a small town with no subway system, I was overwhelmed with Boston's mass transit system. My biggest fear was getting lost. One really doesn't need a car in these large metro areas.

My main focus was completing assignments and doing that well. To accomplish this, I would need the additional time to sort out my notes and then arrange them in a critical analysis paper. I am so thankful to all the people God sent to help me during my time at EDS. People like the librarian who spent countless hours helping me to get acclimated with the school's library and electronic document system. She was always there for me, and it was usually a Friday when I would reach out to her needing some kind of assistance. She never turned me down and suggested that I wait until Monday.

In the beginning, she taught me how to quote and properly cite resources on a bibliography reference. She was always there for me.

One Friday afternoon, it was late in the day and technically she was off; she asked me to wait until she got home and she would call me back to help with completing my assignment. She was amazing and so full of love. One other person who really stands out to me is my writing professor. She taught me how to organize my thoughts. I would send her a paper, and she would send a statement back asking, "Is this what you are writing about?" I would say to her, "How did you sort all that out?" I took her writing class twice just to make sure that I was learning everything correctly.

These two professors were instrumental in helping to set some foundational teachings that helped me comply with citations in my papers. There was one other person who would help with proofing assignments, and that was my first partner. She proofed my papers to make sure they read well and had an orderly flow. My writing professor used to ask me, "How do you write theology well?" She responded, "You write, then rewrite, and rewrite." The first semester was difficult, but as time went by, I became more confident in my writing abilities and things started to get easier. By the third year, my first partner came up for a visit, and we began to venture out to downtown Boston to see a baseball game and to see some of the attractions. She was a much better navigator, and it was more comfortable traveling in pairs. By this time, my homework assignments had gotten easier, and it allowed us to explore Boston more.

The Power of Liberation and Queer Theology

The Episcopal Divinity School, as I already mentioned, is a progressive seminary whose mission is to liberate the "least of these" (Matthew 25:40 NIV). The school already had a history in making a difference with racism and ordaining women, and the focus now was on the LGBTQ+ community. The curriculum imbued a focus on reaching for an egalitarian world where love leads and not judgment. As I was there, I was introduced to queer theology. Queer theology gave another lens on scripture, especially the "clobber" passages that are used to shame the queer community. Again, this focus helped to liberate the gay community from those narrow religious views that always have a patriarchal lens. The patriarchal lens is steeped with old religious dogma, and it favors the male perspective in culture and family. Of course, in both the Hebrew Testament and the New Testament, women were not given equal rights within the community or family. For the most part, women were seen only for their reproductive capabilities. While there are a few exceptions, women were seldom given names or titles unless they gave birth to a patriarch's son. For the most part, they were invisible. I say all this to highlight the fact that we interpret scripture based on our religious upbringing and social norms.

To further my point about social norms dictating the value of women, we find that the Christian Bible highlights the masculine energy through all the patriarchs. However, many of the Native Americans have a matrilineal society that honors the feminine aspect. One other example is the Minoan civilization in Crete who worshiped a feminine goddess. These are a few examples of how culture biases can influence scripture interpretation. The biblical stories reflect cultural consideration of what is valued and accepted in their particular society. I already mentioned how the Native Americans honored the "two spirited" people who demonstrated both male and female aspects. History is filled with examples of other cultures who value both the feminine and masculine energy equally.

Sadly, in our current society, intersex people (having both male and female reproductive organs) are considered offensive and not normal. The intersex or "two spirit" Native Americans were given tribal jobs as deemed appropriate by the individual. One who physically appeared male but identified more with the feminine aspect was assigned to weaving instead of hunting.

While I was at seminary, initially, I focused on liberating the gay community from oppressive scriptures. I focused my studies at the intersection of sexuality and religion. I wanted to help free myself and the gay community from the strict confines of old religious dogma. Studying scriptures from a liberating lens would offer other interpretations of scripture in lieu of the traditional patriarchal and heteronormative lens. We don't realize this, but our families project these conscripted behavioral patterns onto their children. Society labels performance-based behaviors as either masculine or feminine, and anything outside these norms is considered strange and unacceptable. The only way to create an egalitarian society is to begin deconstructing outdated performance based behavioral norms on our children. Let them express themselves as they feel comfortable, even if they refuse to identify strictly as male or female. Many young people are beginning to see themselves as gender nonconforming. This is refreshing and very freeing to those who need flexibility to be who they are at any given moment.

The only way to live fully is to live into our full authentic self. No matter how community may judge us. I believe that the gay community came in during this age of Aquarius to teach us how to love differences or those things outside social acceptance. When we live in fear, we lose the opportunity to accomplish the reason why we came here, and that is to challenge social norms on what it considers lovable. We came here to stretch people's ideas of what love is and to teach that love is love. When one begins breaking down scripture outside the oppressive lens of patriarchy, one can finally understand how scripture is misunderstood in our current age. These writings were written in an oppressive era, and the literal interpretation are not in alignment with deeper truths.

Although scripture can offer us insight on simple morality issues, such as love our neighbor, give to the poor, and love God, they will never liberate those people who fall outside social norms and the confines of religious beliefs. For the most part, we really do not understand scripture. We take the words literally and have no idea what they are really saying. Most religious institutions use scripture as a weapon to condemn and shun the marginalized. This structure sets up a system whereby institutions get to control who they ordain. If a particular candidate doesn't believe a particular way, the institutions are allowed to remove them from clergy candidacy status, telling them that they are not "clergy" material. What they really mean is that the candidate is an individual deeper thinker who leans on their inner compass to guide them through divine encounters. This intuition is the feminine aspect of the divine. This feminine aspect has been removed from mainstream religious institutions and forgotten. The religious institutions control not only who they ordain but also the theology that is taught. If we never had people who challenged the status quo, we would never have a chance to move humanity forward to a more authentic egalitarian lifestyle like Jesus came to teach.

For those of you who grew up in a religion that condemns your sexuality, I want to suggest that your greatest struggle is not in conforming to the worlds standards but having the inner strength and power to find Onement with the Universal Creator. Remember God is only love and anything outside this is not God. This includes judgment. So, if someone remarks that God loves the sinner but hates the sin, this is a juxtaposition of what our creator embodies which is only love. God does not hate period. God or our Creator is one hundred percent love period.

I would like to take a few minutes and explain some of the so called "clobber passages" that are used from the Christian bible to condemn same sex relationships to help each of you who may be struggling to reconcile your sexuality with scripture.

But first, I would like to remind us that Jesus tells us in John 4:24 (RSV) that God is spirit. "God is spirit and those who worship him must worship in spirit and truth". This scripture is revealing to those 'who have ears to hear' that we must begin to study and meditate on the spiritual aspect if we are interested in ascending spiritually. The spiritual word is what liberates the soul from physical matter.

Another scripture that supports Jesus's comment here is Galatians 4:24 (RSV) where the Apostle Paul is talking with the Galatians and explaining this very concept. He is explaining to them that Abraham had two son's one from a slave woman and one from a free woman. He goes on to say that the son born of the slave woman (Hagar) was born according to the flesh (death) and the son born to Sarah represents spiritual life. In Galatians 4:24 St. Paul explains to the Galatians that this story must be understood as an allegory. Figuratively this scripture explains that Hagar represents the slavery to the literal law and it brings death but Sarah represents the promise of spiritual life and brings eternal life with God.

Now that I have quoted a couple of scriptures which encourages us to look at scripture from a spiritual lens, I would like to explain Leviticus 18:22 (RSV). It reads "You shall not lie with a man as with a woman; it is an abomination."

Spiritually when scripture refers to gender it is discussing our energetic qualities. The masculine energy refers to our minds, and the feminine energy refers to our emotions. We are to purify these energetic qualities in our bodies. We are to make them equal or as one. Jesus clearly balanced both his masculine and feminine energies. Jesus demonstrated the higher Christ mind in many stories especially when dealing with religious and government authorities.

However, he also displayed love and compassion in many of the stories. When a man lies with a man as with a woman it implies that he is only working from his masculine energetic qualities of human intellect and reasoning. When he does this, he is leaving out the higher feminine qualities of intuition, love, compassion, and inner guidance.

When these energetic systems are not balanced it is an abomination. We can also understand this as idolatry because we are only listening to our limited human understanding and shutting out higher truths from God. The man (mind) is to unite with the higher feminine (emotions). This is why scriptures tells us that "a man leaves his father and mother and is united to his wife, and they become one flesh (Genesis 2:24, NIV). To receive God's wisdom, we are to listen to both our higher minds and our higher emotions of love and compassion. Does this make sense? This verse has nothing to do with same sex relationships.

Shall we do one more? What about Romans 1:24-27 (NIV)

24 Therefore God gave them over in the sinful desires of their hearts to sexual impurity for the degrading of their bodies with one another.25 They exchanged the truth about God for a lie and worshiped and served created things rather than the Creator—who is forever praised. Amen.

26 Because of this, God gave them over to shameful lusts. Even their women exchanged natural sexual relations for unnatural ones.27 In the same way the men also abandoned natural relations with women and were inflamed with lust for one another. Men committed shameful acts with other men and received in themselves the due penalty for their error.

Once we begin to understand the spiritual meaning of scripture, we can apply this to all scripture. To understand this scripture, we must go back to Romans 1:21-23 "21 For although they knew God, they neither glorified him as God nor gave thanks to him, but their thinking became futile and their foolish hearts were darkened.22 Although they claimed to be wise, they became fools 23 and exchanged the glory of the immortal God for images made to look like a mortal human being and birds and animals and reptiles.

We can see that this verse speaks about humankind knowing of God but they never took the time to give honor or praise. Nor did they find time to meditate on scripture to gain divine wisdom. Because humankind dismissed God's wisdom, they became futile, and their hearts were darkened. We gain spiritual wisdom and truth through God's divine energy. When we dismiss our Creator's divine aspect of knowing all things, we are claiming to be wiser than God. In other words, we exchanged the creator's wisdom for our limited understanding. When we elevate our thoughts and beliefs above God, we are engaging in idol worship. This happens especially in religious institutions where false dogma, creeds, and theology replace God's divine truth.

Romans 1:24-27 above tells us that God gave them over to shameful lusts. Even their women exchanged natural sexual relations for unnatural ones in the same way that men also abandoned natural relations with women and were inflamed with lust for one another. Men committed shameful acts with other men and received in themselves the due penalty for their error. This scripture implies that these people were dismissing God's wisdom, they were putting themselves above God. This is considered idol worship meaning that they were worshiping false ideas. They were invested in their own minds which were depraved because it lacked the wisdom of God's truth. We have free will to follow our own darkened and depraved minds or to listen inwardly to God's divine truth. This group of people chose "lust" or they chose to lie with their own ideas and concepts above God. This act will block us from receiving God's truths or the Christ within.

When we begin to read scripture from a spiritual lens it offers us understanding about what we need to do in order to return to source. We are tasked with merging our masculine and feminine qualities. This is done by transforming our bodies to light bodies or heavenly bodies as Paul tells us. When scripture is mistranslated it creates an insider and outsider effect. Meaning that we judge others as not good enough to belong in the fold. This kind of thinking is humankinds non-loving ways. These ways are not God's ways. God loves us unconditionally.

While in seminary, I was introduced to both liberation theology and queer theology, and those helped me to understand how social norms and cultural biases can skew biblical interpretation. It is our prejudices, lack of understanding, lack of achieving the Christ consciousness, that keeps us judging others while elevating ourselves. My studies at the Episcopal Divinity School taught me how our individual biases can skew God's scripture. Even in my own walk, I asked God, "How can love be wrong?" My Catholic background was holding me back from embracing the real me. My religious roots taught me that I was an abomination and going to hell. These kinds of lower thoughts pull us down and stand our way of claiming our real power. It would take decades before I finally freed myself from the shackles of my past religious untruths.

We are not given an exact road map to our earthly destination or call. It unfolds every single day. This is accomplished by the decisions we make as we follow God. One day we may be heading one way, and then the next day our compass is adjusted to reflect more correctly our purpose. We have no idea how our current experiences may influence tomorrow, the next day, or ten years from now.

Initially, when I began seminary, I was confident where God was leading me. In my deepest heart, I felt God leading me to the gay community to help liberate my people. While in seminary, I immersed myself in queer theology and liberation theology to prepare for my ministry to free the LGBTQ+ people. I graduated from EDS in May 2016 and spent my last year of seminary in conjunction with a clergy internship program. The clergy intern program was a rigorous and a precise program that offered a multitude of hands-on and practical experiences in a clergy role. This final practicum would serve as my last credits for graduation and fulfill my requirements for ordination. I was immersed in clergy life with real church pastoral responsibilities. I experienced many facets of what a pastor would experience to include preaching, worship coordinating, Bible studies, board meetings, weddings, etc. At this point, I was still following spirit.

In life, we are not given our entire plan. All we are given is our intuition to follow our higher calling, and if we are persistent in following this higher calling, we will find our called purpose. I stayed in this position a little longer than I had expected to help fill a pastor vacancy. As the position ended in September 2016, I finally returned home to wait for spirit's next move.

I want to add here that in order to fulfill the soul's plans here in the physical, the individual must learn how to differentiate the personality from the soul. The goal is to blend the higher personality with the higher soul functions. To do this effectively, we must be able to distinguish the soul from the ego. This is every soul's mission while in the physical. Because we operate in 3D, we need our physical functions to process daily affairs while on earth.

I was looking forward to some time off. School was demanding and so was the clergy internship program. I used this downtime to reconnect with family and rest. It was nice not having to write papers or a sermon every week. I wasn't sure where God was leading me next, but I didn't feel as if God was leading me too far from home. I would spend the next several months preparing for my ordination. I would spend my downtime creating ordination liturgy and seeking meaningful music that would accompany the ordination rite. I chose three songs that really spoke to my soul and invited those closest to me to sing and play instruments during the service. I also invited my mentor to lead the service and another friend to preach. It was a beautiful ceremony, and so many of my friends and family came to witness the ordination. It was beautiful. I was ordained on February 18, 2018, and it was a surreal experience. People closest to me helped prepare a memorable experience. The day was a spiritual high. Some said I was glowing. These aspirations are evidence of attaining a spiritual connection to the divine and help us to know we are in alignment with universe.

Although I had already completed the last requirements of ordination, I still didn't know exactly where spirit was leading me next. I remained open to spirit's prompting and waited for guidance and direction. At this point, I still didn't know where all this was leading me. I just kept following my intuition. Ever since I answered my call and began seminary, I just had this deeper inner knowing that these past five years were leading me to a greater purpose. I couldn't articulate exactly what that looked like, but I just kept believing that I was here for a special purpose. As I mentioned, I thought this call was preaching to the gay community, but things unfolded a little bit differently from what I had expected.

A Divine Appointment

True to the universe's way of spontaneity, I received a phone call in May 2018 in which the caller was inviting me to preach at their church. I accepted the offer and initially believed that I would only be there short term—a few months at the longest. I began filling their pulpit on Sundays and remained open to God's direction. We never know where circumstances are leading us. Our job is to embrace each experience and learn our intended lessons. As indicated, I initially began filling the pulpit and was responsible for Sunday sermons. The congregation was actively seeking a full-time pastor but was divided on the final choice. This situation caused an energy shift to occur within the church. As energy begins to shift to higher frequencies, lower energies that are no longer beneficial begin to dissipate. While I didn't understand it at that time, I can now clearly see the evidence of this energy shift.

If we can learn how to see chaos in our lives as early warning signs of energy shifts, we can begin to prepare for higher vibrational changes. This shift can be turbulent as lower and higher energies begin to converge. My stay there exceeded a few months, and a few months would soon become a year, and still there was no sign of the arrival of a permanent pastor. I was dedicated to this church and wanted to see it succeed, so I kept showing up hoping for a miracle. Something deep within me felt that this situation was deeper. After two years, it was obvious that there was no incoming pastor on the horizon. At this point, I had to adjust to more long-term goals for the church. It takes a long time for old, stagnant energy to dissipate. Old energy like the ego is resistant to change.

There is nothing constant in our life but change. Everything is changing, reforming, and adjusting, and if isn't doing this, it will soon die. This includes the church. Everything in our universe changes. This of course also includes humans. We must change and merge with the higher frequencies that the universe sends our way. Even if this convergence seems chaotic and turbulent, a shift is on the horizon regardless of which energetic wave we choose. The two energetic fields will manifest differently in our lives. The higher vibrations will manifest as joy and abundance, and the lower vibrations will manifest a belief system of duality, lack, and separation. I would have never imagined that the turbulence during this time was a result of the different energies colliding. This unfolding began to reveal my higher purpose, and I began to pull from a higher power that I never realized I possessed.

CHAPTER NINE

Spiritual Awakening

As a result of this resonance, I experienced a spiritual awakening. This experience removed a veil within my psyche and led me to an enlightenment. The only way that I know how to describe this experience is through the words of the apostle Paul. He wrote in Acts 9:18 that the scales had fallen from his eyes. This happened on his way to Damascus to kill the Christians, but then suddenly he was transformed and "saw" the higher mysteries. Because of this conversion, his name was changed from Saul to Paul and he went on to accomplish his higher purpose of spreading the good news to the Gentiles.

This transformation is a result of gaining higher consciousness, which leads to an awakening that liberates our souls from this 3D limiting space called earth. We suddenly recognize that the way to liberation is through gaining spiritual wisdom and understanding. This is accomplished when we awaken to the higher truths. Many of you reading this book are searching for answers and a way forward to free yourselves trapped by this world of illusions. Liberation is through finding your higher selves by following your compass of intuition. This intuition sits in a higher plane and requires us to sit quietly and receive its wisdom and guidance.

I found my purpose and power through a spiritual awakening. This transformation was not gained through religious dogma. It wasn't even gain through my master's degree in divinity. There are many paths to enlightenment. Learn to embrace your own truths and never ascribe to someone else's understanding of the path. Lean on your own understanding. It will guide you to your true identity and to your higher purpose on this planet. Until I experienced my awakening, I had no concept of the higher spiritual planes that existed within each of us. The only realms that I understood were this place called earth, a place where God resides, and the underside. I wasn't aware that I was acting from my lower nature. By this I mean that I bought into the concept that living as a lesbian was inherently wrong. If I had never followed that still, small voice within me, I would have never embraced my authentic identity as a lesbian. I would have lived my life as a lie. I would have missed an opportunity to share hope and liberation to so many who are living in fear. I was looking at life through my emotions instead of gaining insight from my higher consciousness

My hope to all those reading this book is to realize that you have a power that sits deep within you and it lies dormant until you are ready to explore it. For those out there who are being ridiculed for not fitting into a mainstream binary society, know that you came here for this exact reason: to show humanity that love is love. You came here to brave the ridicule so that you could bring love and acceptance to this planet. You came here to move this planet forward in love and acceptance. I want you to know that you are a brave soul for embracing a challenging experience that you knew would be difficult and dark. You came here to shine in dark places. I want to encourage all of you to follow your intuition regardless of all the doubters. Know that your path will be difficult and arduous but you know the way, so lean on your higher knowing.

My hope in sharing my awakening journey is to help many of you who feel lost and out of sorts with life. Please do not compare yourselves to other souls. The planet is filled with different vibrations. You are uniquely different and what you have to offer the world is different from the next person. Find your vibration and tune into it. What you are looking for is already inside you. All you have to do is uncover it. To accomplish this, you must understand that this journey is spiritual and not religious. The world needs more light workers to help it evolve into the fifth density. Humanity is at a crossroad and needs the light that you shine to help it transition into the next higher phase.

Try not to focus on the pain and hurt that you will experience. Know that this pain and experience will direct you where you need to go. Learn the lesson in each of your experiences, and keep moving. Try not to assign blame. You will change the world through your love and light, not through judgment, hate, or anger. Let all this go and work on your inner self, releasing any trauma that may be lingering. Work through love and release all anger. Remember our actions and words create our world.

I want to leave you with a knowledge that you are not alone on this journey. Your spirit guides and the council are leading you. You chose to come into this world to make a difference in people's lives. But first, you must find that divine spark deep within you and then learn how to nurture it and feed it. The unfolding will lead you to a spiritual awakening. Seek and find the answers to all your questions. Seek those who have gone before you. Seek the Masters. Know that the universe is supporting you and sending love and light to uplift you along your journey. Remember you are a spiritual individual having a physical experience. Reframe from getting stuck in the physical or the five senses. You are greater and more powerful in the spiritual than the physical. Learn to tap into this power. It is a wellspring of wisdom and knowledge. Listen and follow its lead. It knows where it is leading you: the liberation of your soul!

CHAPTER TEN

Final Encouraging Words

Good luck to all of you who have courageously come here to shine your light and love to help make this world a better place. The journey is challenging, but it is also rewarding, especially to those who boldly live into that authentic self. May you be divinely inspired to finish your journey to enlightenment.

Love and light.

Printed in the United States
by Baker & Taylor Publisher Services